The Early Childhood Planner

Year-Round Activities and Ideas

Pamela Ramsay and Susan Gold

▲▼ Addison-Wesley Publishing Company

Menlo Park, California • Reading, Massachusetts • New York
Don Mills, Ontario • Wokingham, England • Amsterdam • Bonn
Sydney • Singapore • Tokyo • Madrid • San Juan • Paris
Seoul • Milan • Mexico City • Taipei

This book is a publication of the Alternative Publishing Group.

Managing Editor: Diane Silver
Project Editor: Rachel Farber
Production Manager: Janet Yearian
Production Coordinator: Leanne Collins
Design Manager: Jeff Kelly
Illustrations: Rachel Gage

ISBN 0-201-81784-5
2 3 4 5 6 7 8 9-CRS-98 97 96 95 94 93

About the Authors

Susan Gold

Dedication

To my mom, Sylvia Weinstein, who adored little children. And to my parents, Sylvia and Gus Weinstein, who together gave us what all children deserve. . . love, respect, tenderness, and humor.

Biography

Susan Gold lives in Ottawa, Canada, with her husband and two daughters. Her teaching experience includes day care, public school, and English as a Second Language. Susan co-authored *Kidding Around Ottawa*, a resource book for parents, and *Canada Kids' Calendar*, a children's activity calendar. She is actively involved in alternative education.

Pamela Ramsay

Dedication

To my husband and best friend, Gord, for supporting me in everything I do, to my children who inspired me in my choice of vocation, and to my parents who have always encouraged me.

Biography

Pamela Ramsay lives in Ottawa, Canada, with her husband and two grown children. She is an Early Childhood educator with experience in Nursery School and English as a Second Language. She owns the Preschool Store and Future Resources, which supply books, toys, and resources to teachers and parents. Books are her hobby as well as her business.

Table of Contents

Monthly Activities

Dear Teachers

WELCOME TO *THE EARLY CHILDHOOD PLANNER!* This easy-to-use book offers a multitude of seasonal and multicultural ideas, theme and activity center suggestions, and reproducible pages that enable you to create and maintain a well-planned program.

Although the format has changed, our goals remain the same: to help you, the teacher, meet the challenge of providing an exciting, creative, and organized facility for young children.

HERE ARE SOME OF THE FEATURES OF *THE EARLY CHILDHOOD PLANNER...*

• DAILY, WEEKLY, and MONTHLY reproducible planning pages provide plenty of write-in space to help you set goals, organize, implement, and evaluate your program. When placed in a binder, these pages will establish a permanent record for current planning, as well as a sound reference for future planning.

• DAY-AT-A-GLANCE provides space for all the necessary components of a well-rounded early childhood program with room to set goals, plan curriculum, and evaluate activities. We encourage you to incorporate multicultural holidays and other special days into your daily planning.

• WEEK-AT-A-GLANCE gives you an overview of the week to come with extra space for reminders and special notes. Use this page not only to keep abreast of your current week, but also to lay the groundwork for the upcoming week, such as necessary purchases or phone calls.

• MONTH-AT-A-GLANCE presents an overview of the entire month, with enough space to write in special events, activities, and holidays. This page also encourages you to take early preliminary action for activities you are planning for the upcoming month. You may wish to send this page home at the beginning of each month, to inform families of your program plans, special projects, and events for the month to come.

• MONTHLY ACTIVITY PAGES emphasize the special features of each season, including special holidays, and offer an array of activity suggestions for crafts, games, songs, poems, fingerplays, and recipes to share with children. One page in each monthly section presents activity suggestions planned around a special multicultural event .

• ADDITIONAL IDEA PAGES include classroom tips, recommended books, a song list, crafts, and microwave recipes.

- SPECIAL THEME PAGES add an extra dimension to your program planning. They include the following:
  - a section on caring for the environment, with ideas and suggestions for recycling and reusing materials in the classroom and outdoors, as well as activities that encourage an appreciation of nature
  - a section on children's authors with suggested readings and related activities
  - suggestions for creative activities with paint
  - explorations of the properties of water and sand
  - a section on neighborhood outings to augment the outdoor activities that are already a regular part of your program
  - a feature on family involvement enhancing the link between home and school

- All FORMS, along with your planning pages, are reproducible and can be easily posted. They are meant to increase your efficiency, while facilitating recordkeeping, regulationkeeping, and communication with families. Forms include a menu, daily timetable, and fire-drill procedure; theme, birthday, telephone number, meeting note, and inventory pages; a class list; field trip and attendance forms; health problem and allergy lists; and accident reports and emergency phone numbers.

- Holidays and multicultural festivals are included in *The Early Childhood Planner* to help you expand children's sensitivity to the cultural variety in their own communities and beyond. Infuse these festivals into your daily programming to increase appreciation of children's own and others' heritage.

The convenient, compact format of *The Early Childhood Planner* allows you to create your personal planning guide. Simply photocopy the pages that you need, fill them out as required, and place them in a three-ring binder in the order that suits you. Your planner is practical as a current program planner and as a personal time management organizer. When the year is complete, store your planner close at hand as a quick reference for all future planning.

As teachers, we understand the importance of organized planning for you and stimulating activities for the children. *The Early Childhood Planner* provides the framework and content you require to offer a truly professional early childhood program. Please let us know how the planner has been helpful to you. We welcome your suggestions for future editions as well.

Most of all, ENJOY THE CHILDREN!

Pamela Ramsay

Susan Ford

The Benefits Of Good Planning

Efficient planning will improve your program, your interpersonal relationships, and your professional self-image. Planning will help you to keep track of important information; set, meet, and evaluate priorities and objectives; improve communication; and make better use of your time.

Planning benefits the children in your care and their families, the teachers and other people with whom you work, and, of course, you. Once you make the time to plan, you will find that you have more time at your disposal.

By taking the time to plan, you will lessen your workload. You will go to meetings prepared, and fulfill all of your obligations on time. Most important, you will be freer to give your best to the children.

How to Plan

The first step is to delegate a specific time every week to plan. Half an hour to an hour each week is a good start. Some teachers like to (and have time to) build planning time into their workday. Others prefer to work at home.

Photocopy the month-, week-, and day-at-a-glance pages from *The Early Childhood Planner* for at least a three-month period. Put the pages into a large three-ring binder, using dividers to separate the months. Begin each month with the activity pages for that month. They will be useful in planning your week-to-week activities.

Develop your planning strategy in stages, and gradually build on previous planning practices.

STAGE I . . . For the first few weeks, mark in all time- or date-sensitive activities, such as birthdays, holidays, or special activities, on the month-at-a-glance and week at-a-glance pages. Fill in as many of these activities and special occasions for the coming months as you can. Use these pages every week to coordinate time commitments. Write your daily activities, including meetings, professional activities, program themes, and class activities on the week-at-a-glance pages for the next two or three weeks. Use the day-at-a-glance page to plan your curriculum and appointments. Use the blank space to fine-tune this page to your own program.

STAGE II . . . Fill in all information sheets, such as the class list, health notes, allergies list, emergency numbers, field trip personal information, substitute teacher list, and birthdays list. Place all other forms into your binder so that all your planning material is together and at your fingertips.

STAGE III . . . Fill in and post all information that you wish to share with others, such as emergency numbers, fire drill procedure and map, menus, daily timetable, and this week's activities. As you continue to plan, you will require some of the other forms, such as home/school communication records, meeting notes, shopping list, etc.

STAGE IV . . . Now that you have begun your short-term planning and are keeping track of important information, it is time to do some long-term planning for yourself and the children. Arrange with your staff or supervisor to plan time in the next few weeks to conduct observations in the classroom. With the information you gain, set some overall program goals based on the needs and interests of the individuals within your group. As you plan weekly, keep these goals in mind, and build them into your program. For example, you may notice in your planning that you are not doing as many multicultural activities as you wish. Thus, you may decide to add at least one multicultural activity every week, put tales from other countries in the book center, and arrange for visitors to tell the children about a variety of cultures.

Setting Goals

Take the time to set program goals, keep them in mind, and write them down. Here are some tips for meeting your goals.

- Put your goals in writing. This process focuses your thinking and helps ensure that your goals are realistic. Be specific. Write "Plan one hands-on science activity every week," instead of "Do more hands-on science with the children."

- List action steps related to your goals. For example:
  1. Buy one good hands-on science book.
  2. Set up a science table.
  3. Have staff choose activities and construct a schedule.
  4. Post activities and name of staff responsible on board.

- Set deadlines such as, "Start first activity four weeks from today."

- Evaluate. Did you complete each of the steps? Do the children enjoy the activities? If you have not met your goal, why not? What can you do to achieve success?

How to Delegate

Delegation may seem difficult, but coworkers, parents, and other volunteers can be extremely useful in helping you implement your program plans. Just think of delegation of tasks as "asking for help." Here is an example of how you might delegate the preparation work if you were planning four field trips for the year.

1. Plan BEFORE you delegate. Prepare a list of the four field trips, with dates and telephone numbers to give to your helper(s). Photocopy four copies of the Field Trips form.

2. Decide whom to ask for assistance. Think about how much time will be needed, whether the job must be done at the school or can be done elsewhere, and what

skills the person doing the job will need. With this particular example, a working parent could complete this task during a lunch hour. The volunteer would need access to a telephone, and should have strong interpersonal skills.

3. Outline the task in writing. Be very clear about what you would like done and when you need it completed. Make two copies of the job description, one for your file, and one for your volunteer. In this example, the volunteer would phone the four field trip destinations and fill in as much pertinent information as possible.

4. Manage and evaluate. Check in with your volunteer regularly to see if everything is running smoothly. When the job is complete, ask for input in evaluating the task. Did the volunteer have the necessary information? Did it take a longer or shorter amount of time than expected? Are there any suggestions for next year's volunteer? Put all suggestions in writing and use them to refine the job for next year.

5. Reward. You can thank your volunteer in many ways: a personal note, flowers, a small gift, acknowledgment in the school newsletter or on the bulletin board, or a "volunteer appreciation" event for all volunteers who have helped make your job easier. You may wish to include the children in planning a celebration.

Some Planning Tricks

- For future reference, save all of your plans, notes, letters to parents, etc. from year to year. If you have a computer or a volunteer with a computer, store notes and letters on disk, so that they can be easily changed, updated, or improved.

- Use colored paper clips to mark pages pertaining to the current week or day.

- Use highlighters to highlight important dates, designating different colors for different topics. For example, highlight all birthdays in pink, planning time in yellow, and appointments in green. Be creative with color!

- Take a large brown envelope the same size as your binder, and punch three holes down one side. Put this envelope in your binder to hold important bits of paper and other miscellaneous items.

Planning is a form of stress management. Use our planning pages as a personal day-timer, not just a curriculum planner. A good plan allows you to focus your time, energy, and resources on the areas that you have decided are most important. With organized planning, you will have confidence and a sense of achievement when your days run smoothly.

Daily Timetable

Group _____

Time a.m.	Activity

Time p.m.	

Day-at-a-glance

Activity	Plan	Goals	Evaluation
Circle Time			
Creative			
Cognitive			
Dramatic			
Gross Motor			
Fine Motor			

Reminders

Week-at-a-glance

	MONDAY	TUESDAY	WEDNESDAY	THURSDAY	FRIDAY
a.m.					
p.m.					

Saturday _____

Sunday _____

Notes _____

Month-at-a-glance

MONDAY	TUESDAY	WEDNESDAY	THURSDAY	FRIDAY

Family Involvement

Parents and other family members are an invaluable resource to you and your classroom. Family members can contribute to your program by helping in class, chaperoning on field trips, sitting on committees, or doing small jobs at home. Children benefit immeasurably by the strong link that develops between home life and school life.

Although parents will be deeply involved in your program, all adults in the children's lives can contribute to the program's success. There is nothing quite like the relationship that builds between grandparents and children. Encourage children to bring their grandparents around. Aunts, uncles, caregivers, siblings, college students, and other community members can also deeply enrich children's school experiences.

Why Involve Families?
- Children feel special on the days that family members spend time in class.
- Children feel valued when families show interest in their school program.
- Children benefit from the extra attention of additional adults.
- Children learn to adapt to a variety of adults.
- All children benefit from the experience and expertise of family members.

Other Benefits:
- Staff have extra time to spend with individual children.
- Family presence helps staff to better understand the backgrounds of the children.
- Family and staff members benefit from the collegial relationship that develops when they work together.
- Family members can observe how the children function at school.
- Family members not only get to know children's teachers and playmates, but they also build a rapport with staff.
- Family members have opportunities to chat with staff about the children.
- Family members can build skills at school that enhance their interaction at home.
- Observing other children helps family members to appreciate the developmental stages through which their own children are progressing.

How Can Working Family Members Contribute to Your Program?
"It's O.K. to come and play. . ."
A teacher we know has this open-door policy for parents and other family members to drop in whenever they have available time. This encouragement for adults to come to school for a relaxing visit, to play or just observe, builds their confidence about participating in the program, and builds the relationship between family and school.

When family members are inclined to contribute to your program, how can they arrange time away from work to get there? There are several possibilities, some requiring cooperation on the part of employers and/or colleagues:

- During the work/schoolday, ANY amount of time parents can spend in class is welcome. So. . . a few minutes in the morning to share a puzzle or read a storybook before going off to work, the occasional lunch hour taken at school, or some time to participate in a game before rushing home for dinner are all valuable.

- Employers are becoming more understanding about the requirement for "family time," and will often be flexible about rearranging time, or using mental health days for family members to take time to attend school for a visit, special activity, or half-day field trip. With advance planning, family members can arrange to adjust hours or trade a shift with a colleague.

- A family member who works odd hours may be able to visit during the schoolday.

- With the help of supportive teachers, some very creative solutions for involving family members in the daytime have been discovered.

At Night

- This is an opportunity for parents and other family members to contribute at home by doing small jobs for teachers, such as cutting and pasting for planned activities. Encourage family members to invite children to help with these jobs.

- Some family members can find their niche by serving on committees. Meetings and planning sessions usually, if not always, take place at night. Parents may have to work out care arrangements with other family members, neighbors, or babysitters. If meetings are planned early enough in the evening, some parents will bring their children along, and an older sibling or neighborhood teenager can care for children in one room while parents and other family members meet in another. Committee work has social, as well as program-related, benefits.

Weekends

- Social and fund-raising activities, such as garage sales or fun fairs, often occur on weekends. This is a much less harried time, when parents and children can partici-pate in school-related activities together. Families have the opportunity to social-ize and work together to benefit the children's school, and many friendships have been known to sprout under these circumstances.

- Weekends can be a good time for committee meetings. Child care is more readily available on weekends, and family members with busy weekday schedules may be able to participate more often.

- Arrange workdays on occasional weekends—perhaps one per season—to paint lockers, reorganize cupboards, build equipment, or do a spring cleaning. Order in pizza, or have a potluck dinner afterwards.

Encouraging Family Involvement

In many cases neither staff nor families are accustomed to family involvement in school programs; it may take a while for everyone to become comfortable with the idea. Family involvement works only when the staff is committed to the idea that it is best for the program and for the children.

- Start slowly with invitations for parents or other family members to make short visits or to do specific jobs. As you get to know each other in the school setting, family members and teachers will learn how best to use available time.

- Be honest with family members about your needs and expectations so they can best fulfill their role as partners in the implementation of your program.

- Posted worksheets enable visitors to come in and get right down to business.

- If you have a visit arranged, make a phone call the previous night or engage in a brief chat at pickup time to share expectations for the next day.

- Encourage family members to talk to you about how they perceive their role in the program. This sort of regular communication can prevent potential confusion.

- Arrange evaluation sessions with family members regarding their volunteer activities. Take this time to share ideas and get suggestions from family members on change and improvement of jobs.

- Be patient. It takes time to develop a good working model of a family involvement program. You are looking for a balance between what a parent feels able to contribute, and your expectations as a teacher. Honest communication is the key.

A Final Note:

There are unequalled benefits for your children when families and teachers work together to contribute to the school program. If you haven't yet started to involve families in your program, we encourage you to give it a try.

Registration Form

Child's Name _____ Birthdate _____

Address _____ Age _____

Parent/Guardian _____ Parent/Guardian _____

Address _____ Address _____

Phone _____ Phone _____

Place of work _____ Place of work _____

Emergency contact _____
                                      name   telephone

Relationship to child _____

Child's doctor _____ Phone _____

Program _____ Starting date preferred _____

Days per week: Mon. _____ a.m. Tues. _____ a.m. Wed. _____ a.m. Thurs. _____ a.m. Fri. _____ a.m.

Full week: _____ _____ p.m. _____ p.m. _____ p.m. _____ p.m. _____ p.m.

Evenings: _____ Weekends: _____

Siblings (names/ages) _____

Other programs attended _____

Is your child toilet-trained?   Yes _____   No _____

I am available to help: Never _____   Occasionally _____   Frequently _____

Parent/Guardian Signature _____ Date: _____

OFFICE USE ONLY

Medical form provided?   Yes _____ No _____ Full fee paying _____

Registration fee received?   Yes _____ No _____ Eligible for subsidy?   Yes _____ No _____

Start date _____ Withdrawal date _____

Date _____

Dear Family:

Please share some information with me about your child. You have valuable insights that will help me provide the best possible environment for learning. I would like to develop a partnership between home and school and encourage you to share both your child's achievements and any concerns you may have. Please fill in this form and send it to school with your child.

Parent/Guardian _____   Parent/Guardian _____

Address _____   Address _____

Business phone _____   Business phone _____

Home phone _____   Home phone _____

Best time to call _____   Best time to call _____

Languages spoken _____

Child's special interests _____

_____

_____

_____

_____

_____

Child's special needs _____

_____

_____

_____

_____

 # Take-Home Authorizations

Take-Home Authorization

I authorize _____

authorized person

to pick up my child _____ on

child's name

_____   _____

pickup date   description

_____   _____

staff signature

_____   _____

date   parent signature

Take-Home Authorization

I authorize _____

authorized person

to pick up my child _____ on

child's name

_____   _____

pickup date   description

_____   _____

staff signature

_____   _____

date   parent signature

Volunteers

Name	Specialty	Address	Phone	Time Available

Dear Family:

Your junk may be our treasure! The following list includes some of the materials we use to enhance your child's learning throughout the year. We would really appreciate it if you'd send along any "treasures" you have for our room.

- fabric, trim
- newspapers, catalogs, magazines
- assorted cans, plastic containers, bottles, etc.
- buttons, spools
- road maps
- shells
- lids, bottle caps
- keys
- nuts and bolts
- seeds
- floor tiles
- wallpaper books and pieces
- beads
- paper rolls
- old socks
- egg cartons

- aluminum plates
- wood scraps
- coat hangers
- boxes — all kinds
- old cutlery
- muffin tins
- old pantyhose
- measuring spoons and cups
- wooden sticks, tongue depressors
- old radios, clocks, small appliances
- old costume jewelry
- old clothing for dress-up
- posters — travel, grocery store, etc.
- old greeting cards
- pipe cleaners

JUST A NOTE

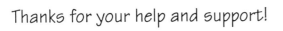

To _____

_____

_____

_____

_____

_____

_____

_____

| signed | date |

In Appreciation

To _____

Thanks for your help and support!

_____

_____

_____

_____

From _____

Environment

Things You Can Do with Preschoolers for a Cleaner, Healthier Environment

In addition to reducing, recycling, and reusing materials, one of the most important steps to take with young children is to encourage in them an appreciation of nature. It may be difficult to do all of the things listed below, but you can pick two or three things and do them well. You and the children can make a difference. Use the list of recommended books and games at the end of this section to supplement the activities.

Clean Up Your Playground or Park.

In the spring, take the children out for a cleanup walk. Before your walk, talk about littering, and discuss the kinds of garbage they might expect to find. Point out the dangers of glass and other sharp objects. Tell the children to show those things to an adult — and not pick them up. Give the children each a paper bag to collect the garbage they find. When you return to the classroom, do a group story about the kinds of garbage you have found. Have a small garbage can as part of your play-yard equipment.

Start a Compost Box.

If regulations allow, put a compost box in the corner of your outdoor play area. Have a covered container indoors, and teach the children to put biodegradable garbage in it for addition to the compost. If your situation does not allow this, find a "neighbor" who has a compost box that you can visit and who would welcome additions of material from your school.

Plant a Vegetable Garden.

Have a small vegetable garden in the play yard, or use barrels or large planters for your garden. Perhaps you have a close neighbor who has lots of room but not enough time or energy to look after a garden. This would make a nice cross-generational sharing activity, with the children going in small, manageable groups to work in the garden; the bounty could be shared by all. If this is not possible, plant some quick growing seeds indoors for the children to tend, for example, alfalfa sprouts, lettuce, or chives. If you do not want to chance starting your plants from seeds, take the children on an outing to purchase seedlings. If possible, arrange for a visit to a local garden market.

Respect Growing Things.

Talk about gardens, both private and public, and respect for the things growing there. Teach children not to walk on or run through gardens, and not to pick flowers or plants. Teach them to respect trees, and not to break branches or bark off of trees. When gathering samples for a nature study, collect things that are on the ground. When visiting natural settings, such as a forest or field, teach the children to take only a sample of the more prolific plants or flowers, and teach them which plants and flowers are protected in your area.

Feed the Birds.

Put a bird feeder in the play yard, in a place where it can be safely observed through a window. The birds will not come to the feeder when the children are outside, but will appear at the quieter times of the day, either in the morning or the afternoon. If you are planning to put any new bushes or small trees in your yard, speak to the nursery people about trees that will attract local birds, and still be safe for children. A water source will also encourage the birds. Help the children make small bird feeders that they can take home. REMEMBER THAT IF YOU START TO FEED THE BIRDS IN THE WINTER, THEY WILL DEPEND ON YOU.

Provide Nesting Material for the Birds.

In the very early spring, gather long strands of dead grass and place on the tops of bushes or fences where the birds will find them. Give each child a few strands of light wool or string to put out. Even though you might not see the birds take the materials, you will know by their disappearance that they have been used. If you go for a bird-nest-hunting walk before the leaves appear, you may see some of "your" wool in a bird's nest.

Have a Class Pet.

One of the nicest ways to teach small children to appreciate animals is to have a class or school pet. The children can help with its care and feeding as well as observe its behavior. Fish, hamsters, gerbils, rats, guinea pigs, or small rabbits are very classroom friendly. If you cannot have a pet all year, perhaps you could arrange to "borrow" a pet for a week or a day. Teach the children that not all pets like to be handled — they need quiet time just as we do. Then help the children write a class story about their experiences, or a story about their pets at home.

Cut Down on Disposable Dishes.

For snack or lunch times, use unbreakable, reusable dishes. Put the children's names on their juice cups, and have each child wash his or her own cup. Set up three dish pans, one with warm soapy water and a teaspoon of bleach in it and two with rinse water. Have the children wash their cups, double rinse them, and put them on a rack to dry.* If you go on an outing or a picnic, use paper cups and plates, which are biodegradable, rather than plastic or polystyrene. Then deposit them in appropriate containers.

Recycle.

Collect your glass and aluminum containers for recycling. Put the material in a recycling box if there is a program in your area, or take it once a month to a recycling depot. This activity would make a good field trip.

Teach the children not to use a large piece of paper when a small piece will do. Save scraps of paper or other craft materials to use for collage or other creative projects.

Use Found Materials.

Have families and friends save all recyclable materials for art projects. If you plan well ahead, you can post a list on the bulletin board to let family members know your future needs. Ask the children to help you think of uses for your collection of materials. Put as much of the material as possible on your cut-and-paste shelf for the children to use freely.

*We checked this with our local health official. Please check with the health department in your area to be sure that these instructions meet with their requirements.

Books

(Suggested ages are in parentheses.)

Fiction

The Fisherman and the Bird, Bijou Le Tord. Scholastic, 1984.
When the fisherman goes to take his boat out, he finds that a bird has built its nest in the mast. The fisherman decides to wait for the eggs to hatch, rather than disturb the bird. (3–7)

The Little House, Virginia L. Burton. Houghton Mifflin, 1942
This classic Caldecott Medal winner is the story of a little house in the country swallowed up by urban sprawl, and how it is rescued and returned to the peace of the country. (2–5)

One Step, Two. . . , Charlotte Zolotow. Lothrop, Lee & Shepard, 1981.
A girl and her mother go for a walk to discover the sights of spring, and learn how to appreciate the daffodils without picking them. (2–5)

A Salmon for Simon, Betty Marie Waterton. Atheneum Publishers, 1980.
The story of a Canadian Indian boy and a salmon shows a child's sensitivity towards a living creature and his satisfaction at saving a life. (4–7)

Waiting, Nicki Weiss. Greenwillow Books, 1981.
A little girl discovers the sights, sounds, and smells of nature while waiting for her mother. (3–5)

When Dad Cuts Down the Chestnut Tree, Pam Ayres. Walker Books, 1988.
A family thinks of all the things they will be able to do with the wood when Dad cuts down the chestnut tree. When they list all of the things they would miss, they decide not to cut down the tree after all. (3–7)

When Dad Fills in the Garden Pond, Pam Ayres. Walker Books, 1988.
Mum wants Dad to fill in the pond so they will have more yard. The family begins to remember all that they like about the pond and Mum changes her mind. (3–7)

Wolf Island, Celia Godkin. Fitzhenry & Whiteside, 1990.
The author shows how the balance of nature is affected when a family of wolves accidentally gets removed from their island home. A simple story for your children — with a happy ending. (4–7)

A Wolf Story, David Michael McPhail. Charles Scribner's Sons, 1981.
Based on a true story in London, some children champion a timber wolf and defend his right to live freely. (5–7)

Nonfiction

The Carrot Seed, Ruth Kraus. Harper & Row, 1945.
A little boy learns that it takes patience to grow things. (3–5)

Growing Vegetable Soup, Lois Ehlert. Harcourt Brace Jovanovich, 1987.
A wonderfully colorful book about growing the vegetables to make soup. Now available in paperback. (3–7)

Second Chance Books, Hugh Lewin and Lisa Kopper. Hamish Hamilton, 1989.
Simple stories that focus on the earth and what we can do to help. (3–7)
Four titles in the series:
   A Flower in the Forest
   A Well in the Desert
   A Shell on the Beach
   A Bamboo in the Wind

The Wildlife ABC, Jan Thornhill. Grey de Pencier, 1988. (2–4)
The Wildlife 1, 2, 3, Jan Thornhill. Grey de Pencier, 1989. (4–7)
Two large, colorful books that introduce children to the variety of animals in the world, with some pertinent information about each one.

For the Teacher

Animals in the Classroom, David Kramer. Addison-Wesley, 1989.
Provides suggestions for obtaining and caring for small animals in the classroom, background information on each animal, and interesting activities for the students.

Bugplay: Activities with Insects for Young Children, Marlene Hapai and Leon Burton. Addison-Wesley, 1990.
Shares information about the insect world with children. Includes poems, songs, drawings, and suggestions for hands-on experiences.

Crafts for Fun: Using Recycled & Everyday Items, Virginia Rich and Sandy Bauer. Judson Press, 1986.
Crafts for preschoolers and older children using everything you were going to throw out.

My First Nature Book, Angela Wilkes. Stoddart Publishing, 1990.
A large book with twenty-two activities for children of various ages. Good activities, good instructions. The children will enjoy the pictures.

Nature for the Very Young, Marcia Bawden. John Wiley & Sons, 1989.
Lots of good activities to do with your group of children.

Teachables from Trashables: Homemade Toys that Teach, Emma C. Linderman. Toys 'n Things Press, 1979. *Teachables II: Homemade Toys that Teach,* Rhoda Redleaf. Toys 'n Things Press, 1987.
Turn junk materials into fun and educational toys. Fully illustrated directions, age-group guidelines, suggested play activities, and descriptions of skills children gain.

Games

Here are three board games that young children can play.

A Beautiful Place. For 4- to 7-year-olds. This is a cooperative game in which everyone works together to restore the beauty and ecological balance of the earth. Environmental concepts are presented in a simple way. To order, contact: Family Pastimes, RR4, Perth, Ontario, Canada K7H 3C6.

Harvest Time. Another cooperative game. For 4- to 7-year-olds. Plant your gardens, and then roll the die to find out what to harvest first. Children learn that they can harvest their gardens before winter comes if they work together. To order, contact: Family Pastimes, RR4, Perth, Ontario, Canada K7H 3C6.

Save the Forest. For children 5 and up. As you throw the die and move your piece through the forest, you pick up litter along the way and complete a puzzle showing the habitat of various animals. The winner is the one who accumulates the most points for cleaning up litter. Manufactured by Ravensberger Company, Germany.

Take Off With Books

Books can provide a wonderful springboard to curriculum planning. In this section, we take a look at four children's authors, using each author's style and books as a basis for activities with children. We have offered interesting bits of information about each author for the teacher, as well as information that will appeal to the children. Although some of the books are no longer in print, we have been careful to recommend books that we know are still widely available in libraries.

Margaret Wise Brown

"Brownie," as Margaret Wise Brown was called, was born May 23, 1910, in New York City. Before her death in 1952, she wrote more than 100 books for children. In the late 1930s she pioneered a style of writing for children that focused on their world—on their senses (*The Noisy Book*), their fears (*Runaway Bunny*), and their need for familiarity and stability (*Goodnight Moon*). Her numerous pets, including a dog and more than 30 rabbits, became characters in many of her books. The books still appear on the bestseller lists.

Best-Known Books

The Noisy Book
The Country Noisy Book
The Seashore Noisy Book
The Indoor Noisy Book
The Noisy Bird Book
The Winter Noisy Book
The Quiet Noisy Book
The Summer Noisy Book
Runaway Bunny
Goodnight Moon
The Golden Egg Book
Christmas in the Barn

Activities

Read to the children as many of the *Noisy* books as possible over the period of a week or two. Tell the children that some of the books were written more than 50 years ago, when their grandparents were children. Discuss with the children ways in which their lives are the same or different from the lives of the children in the stories. Note that all of the books are interactive—they encourage responses from the readers. Invite the children to make noises to go with the stories, or to tell what noises the author has included.

- Put out puzzles that picture things that make noise, such as animals, musical instruments, vehicles, people. If you have electronic books with sound effects, include them as well.
- Record a variety of familiar sounds for the children to listen to and identify.
- Put animal cards, pictures, or plastic animals into a bag and have the children take turns drawing a card and acting out the sound made by that animal. The other children guess the animal.
- Make a "Noisy" collage and a "Quiet" collage with pictures cut from catalogs and magazines.

Robert Munsch

Robert Munsch was born June 11, 1945, in Pittsburgh, Pennsylvania; in 1976 he emigrated to Canada. He is primarily a storyteller, who develops his stories through the storytelling process. The development of a story starts when the children ask him to "tell a story about ____." Then, again with the children's help, the author tells and retells the stories before they reach their final form. Munsch's stories give insight into how children view the world, and offer help in solving their problems.

Best-Known Books
Murmel, Murmel
Mud Puddle
David's Father
The Paper Bag Princess

Activities
Read several of Munsch's books to the children over the period of a week. Point out how the author uses sound, onomatopoeia, and repetition to hold the children's interest. Explain to the children how Munsch refined his stories, telling and retelling a story many times before finally putting it in a book.

- To illustrate the author's storytelling process, create a group story on an experience chart. Let the children choose the topic, and make sure that everyone participates.

The next day, read the story to the children and ask if they want to change anything. Don't be afraid to ask leading questions such as: "Is this the way you would feel?" "What do you think happened next?" "Is this the way you want the story to end?" "What would you like to add?" Write several class stories if this is an activity the children enjoy.

When everyone feels satisfied that the story is "finished," give the children large sheets of paper and have them illustrate various aspects of the story. Print the story on the appropriate pages, and add a cover to make a class Big Book. Record the class story, and add it to your tape collection for the listening center.

- Let children experience other ways to enjoy a story by including some of Robert Munsch's records or audio cassettes in your listening center. If your classroom has a video cassette recorder, the children can watch the author tell his own stories.

Ezra Jack Keats

A native of Brooklyn, New York, Ezra Jack Keats was born March 11, 1916. He died in 1983. Keats's stories are about learning situations for children under five years of age as they discover new abilities (*Whistle for Willie*), cope with ambivalent emotions (*Peter's Chair*), and learn new attitudes (*Goggles*). The stories are set in urban America, with the streets the playgrounds and found objects the playthings.

Best-Known Books
The Snowy Day
Whistle for Willie
Jenny's Hat
Peter's Chair
A Letter to Amy
Goggles
Shadows

Activities
Read *The Snowy Day* to the children during cold winter weather, if possible. If your school is in a snowy climate, when the children go outside to play, encourage them to

try some of the things that Peter enjoyed, such as drawing in the snow with a stick, making snow angels, and making footprints forwards, backwards, and sideways. If the weather in your area is too warm for snow, walk around the playground with the children and have them name some of the things Peter might do if he lived in their area.

- Bring a small amount of snow inside and put it in clear containers. Have the children predict how long it will take to melt. What does the snow look like after it melts? Would you want to eat the snow?
- Make a matching game by cutting ten pairs of mittens out of different-colored or patterned paper such as wallpaper samples. Have the children match the pairs. Find examples in the books to show the children how Keats used collage to illustrate his books.
- After reading *Peter's Chair,* have a group discussion about different types of families. Invite the children to talk about how they felt when a sibling was born, how they think their older siblings felt when they were born, or how they think they would feel about the arrival of a new sibling in the family.
- Have the children draw pictures of the members of their family. Have them identify each member while you write a name under the picture.
- Call attention to Keats's different art styles. Then set up your art center for collage (*The Snowy Day*) and shadow painting (*Shadows*). Include a variety of different-colored paper and patterned cloth at the collage table and black, white, and gray tempera paints at the easels.

Virginia Lee Burton

Born in Newton Center, Massachusetts, on August 30, 1909, Virginia Lee Burton produced her books in reverse order compared to the way most other authors work. First she did the illustrations, then she wrote the stories to fit the space that was left on the pages. Her stories are based on objects or machines, with illustrations that are wonderfully detailed and give maplike vistas.

Best-Known Books
The Little House
Katy and the Big Snow
Mike Mulligan and His Steam Shovel
Choo Choo

Activities

Read *The Little House* to the class. Elicit from the children how the Little House feels when things happen to her that she cannot prevent (she feels curious, sad, fearful, lonely, happy). Pay particular attention to the concept of passing time. In this story the children will note the sun rising and setting each day, the moon waxing and waning each month, and the seasons changing each year. They also see the change from country to city, changes in families as members grow older, and changes in clothing styles and methods of transportation over the years.

- Discuss with the children the concept of time: days, weeks, months, and years.
- Ask the children to observe the changes in the moon throughout a month. Help them chart the moon during this period, showing the full moon to new moon and back again. This is best done in the winter when it is dark early enough for young children to observe the moon.
- Read *Katy and the Big Snow* to the class. Be sure to look at the details of the different types of machinery in the frames around each picture.
- Have the children make collages of their favorite machinery and trucks. If they know the names of the equipment, have them tell you as you write the names on each collage.
- Put construction equipment and trucks in the sandbox for the children to use.
- Include construction equipment and trucks in the block center. Encourage the children to use the blocks to re-create one of the scenes from *Katy and the Big Snow*. Masking tape on the carpet or floor makes wonderful roads for the city.
- Place large pieces of craft paper on the floor and tape down the corners. Encourage the children to make "maps," with roads and buildings. A fun way to make the roads is to dip the wheels of a vehicle into a shallow tray of paint, and then "paint" the roads by moving the car along on the paper. Buildings can be drawn on the craft paper or cut out from construction paper and added last.
- Take a walk with the children, pointing out the buildings, streets, and landmarks in the school's neighborhood. Discuss these special landmarks as you help the children create a map of the area.

Recommended Books

Allen, Judy, Earldene McNeil, Velma Schmidt. *Cultural Awareness for Young Children.* Menlo Park, CA: Addison-Wesley, 1992.

Anselmo, Sandra, Pamela Rollins, Rita Shuckman. *R is for Rainbow.* Reading, MA: Addison-Wesley, 1986.

Baratta-Lorton, Mary. *Workjobs: Activity-Centered Learning for Early Childhood.* Reading, MA: Addison-Wesley, 1972.

Baratta-Lorton, Mary. *Workjobs II: Number Activities for Early Childhood.* Reading, MA: Addison-Wesley, 1978.

Calkins, Lucy M. *Lessons from a Child.* Portsmouth, NH: Heinemann, 1983.

Cass-Beggs, Barbara. *Your Baby Needs Music.* Reading, MA: Addison-Wesley, 1990.

Chud, Gyda, and Ruth Fahlman. *Early Childhood Education for a Multicultural Society.* University of British Columbia: Pacific Educational Press, 1985.

Coombs, Ernie, and Shelly Tanaka. *Mr. Dressup's Book of Things to Make and Do.* Toronto, Ontario: CBC Enterprises, 1984.

Cryer, Debbie, Thelma Harms, Beth Bourland. *Active Learning for Twos.* Reading, MA: Addison-Wesley, 1988.

_____ . *Active Learning for Threes.* Reading, MA: Addison-Wesley, 1988.

Graeme, Joceyln, and Ruth Fahlman. *Hand in Hand: Multicultural Experiences for Young Children.* Reading, MA: Addison-Wesley, 1990.

Hohmann, Mary, Bernard Banet, and David Weikart. *Young Children in Action: A Manual for Preschool Educators.* Ypsilanti, MI: High/Scope Press, 1979.

Kingore, Bertie W., and Glenda M. Higbee. *We Care: A Preschool Curriculum for Children Ages 2–5.* Glenview, IL: Scott, Foresman, 1988.

Landsberg, Michele. *Michele Landsberg's Guide to Children's Books.* Markham, Ontario: Penguin Books, 1986.

Nash, Chris. *The Learning Environment: A Practical Approach to the Education of the Three, Four, and Five-Year-Old.* Toronto, Ontario: Collier MacMillan, 1989.

Paasche, Carol, Lola Gorrill, Bev Strom. *Children with Special Needs in Early Childhood Settings*. Reading, MA: Addison-Wesley, 1990.

Rich, Virginia S., and Sandy Bauer. *Crafts for Fun: Using Recycled and Everyday Items*. Valley Ford, PA: Judson Press, 1986.

Schwartz, Susan, and Mindy Pollishuke. *Creating the Child-Centered Classroom*. Toronto, Ontario: Irwin, 1990.

Segal, Marilyn, and Len Tomasello. *Nuts and Bolts: Organization and Management Techniques for an Interest-Centered Preschool Classroom*. Atlanta, GA: Monarch Books, 1981.

Strickland, Dorothy S., and Lesley Mandel Morrow, eds. *Emerging Literacy: Young Children Learn to Read and Write*. Newark, DE: IRA, 1989.

Sutherland, Z., and May Hill Arbuthnot. *Children and Books*. 7th edition. Glenview, IL: Scott, Foresman, 1986.

Trelease, Jim. *The Read-Along Handbook*. Revised Edition. New York: Penguin, 1985.

Van Straalen, Alice. *The Book of Holidays Around the World*. New York: E.P. Dutton, 1986.

Veitch, Beverly, and Thelma Harms. *Cook and Learn—Pictorial Single-Portion Recipes: A Child's Cookbook*. Reading, MA: Addison-Wesley, 1981.

Williams, Leslie, and Yvonne De Gaetano. *Alerta: A Multicultural Bilingual Approach to Teaching Young Children*. Reading, MA: Addison-Wesley, 1985.

 # Microwave Revolution

The availability of the microwave oven opens up many interesting curriculum options for the classroom.

Even if you cannot afford to buy a small microwave oven for your program, you can easily carry your own microwave oven out to your car, into the classroom, and plug it in, for plenty of fun and safe activities with the children. No longer do you have to leave cooking out of the curriculum because you do not have access to a stove. Here are a few things you can do:

Microwave Play Dough

2 cups all-purpose flour
1 cup salt
1/2 cup cornstarch
1 Tbsp. powdered alum
2 cups water
1 Tbsp. oil
food coloring

Mix dry ingredients together in 2-quart glass bowl. Gradually stir in wet ingredients until smooth. Microwave on high (100 percent) power uncovered, 4 to 5 minutes, stirring every minute, until mixture is thick. (Mixture will be quite lumpy.)
Turn onto countertop and allow mixture to cool enough to handle. Knead about 2 minutes, until smooth. Store in airtight containers in refrigerator.

Dried Flowers

Enough brightly colored flowers, half-opened and firm, for each child
Fine white sand ("Super Sand")
One microwave-proof container for each child
One 2-cup glass measure
Water

Cut flower stem 1 inch long. Have each child spread a layer of sand in the bottom of his or her container (about 3/4 inch). Stick flower in sand, bloom up. Gently spoon sand between and over petals, covering flower completely. Place 2-cup glass measure full of water, and container with flower in microwave. Heat at medium-high a few minutes. (See NOTE.) Let stand overnight. Carefully remove, and use for flower arranging or craft.

NOTE: Use the same flower type for each child. Test one a day or so before drying to determine length of time. Here are some guidelines:

Daisies   1/2 to 1 minute
Carnations   2 to 2 1/2 minutes
Cornflowers   3/4 to 1 minute
Small Mums   2 to 2 1/2 minutes
Roses   2 to 3 minutes

Microwave Bread Dough Ornaments

2 cups flour
1 cup salt
1 cup water

Combine dry ingredients, add water slowly, stirring to make a ball. Turn out onto lightly floured surface and knead until smooth, about 7 to 10 minutes. Have children fashion ornaments, by hand or with a rolling pin and cookie cutters. Flat designs, up to 3 by 3 inches, work best. If hanging ornaments, make a hole in the top of the ornament before baking. Use water to moisten slightly if joining one piece of dough to another.

Have children place ornament on a piece of cardboard covered with waxed paper with their name on it. Place ornament on cardboard on the glass oven tray. Heat each piece about 3 to 4 minutes on medium-low. Turn over once during heating if design allows. If a piece starts to bubble, stop the microwave and pierce the bubble with a pin. If a piece starts to curl, stop the microwave and weigh down the curling spot with a piece of microwave-safe glass for 30 seconds. Continue heating. Ornaments can now be painted, stained, sprinkled with glitter, or left plain, and shellacked.

Food

Children can cook many simple recipes in the microwave oven. Use individual recipes and let each child cook his or her own, or prepare a group recipe. Let your imagination be your guide.

Craft Recipes

Cooked Play Dough

1 cup flour
1/2 cup salt
1 cup water
1 Tbsp. vegetable oil
2 tsp. cream of tartar
few drops food coloring

Mix all ingredients in a medium-sized saucepan, tinting to desired color. Heat over medium heat, stirring until ingredients form a ball. Turn onto dry surface and knead when cool enough to touch. Store in a plastic bag. Keeps for about four weeks.

Craft Clay 1

1 cup cornstarch
2 cups salt
1 1/3 cups cold water

Put 2/3 cup water and salt in a saucepan. Bring to a boil. Mix remaining water well with cornstarch. Blend the mixtures together, and knead until well mixed. Store in a plastic bag, refrigerated. Shape and air dry. Paint with tempera and when dry shellac if desired.

Sawdust Dough

5 cups fine sawdust
1 cup wallpaper paste
    (box should be marked safe for children)
4 to 5 cups water

Mix dry ingredients. Add enough water to make a good modelling consistency (forms a ball without cracking). Store in a plastic bag in the refrigerator overnight. Make shapes and dry on rack. Looks like wood.

Uncooked Play Dough

2 cups self-rising flour
2 Tbsp. alum
2 Tbsp. salt
2 Tbsp. cooking oil
1 cup plus 2 Tbsp. boiling water
few drops food coloring

Mix well, turn onto dry surface, and knead. Store in a plastic bag. This dough is nonhardening.

Craft Clay 2

2 cups baking soda
1 cup cornstarch
1 1/4 cups water
few drops food coloring

Mix dry ingredients in saucepan. Add cold water gradually. Heat to boiling, stirring until thick. Turn onto dry surface and knead when cool enough to handle. Store in air-tight container. Dry in 125° to 150° oven.

Squirt Paint

4 cups water
4 cups flour
1 cup salt
1 tsp. tempera powder

Mix ingredients well. Put into plastic bottles with squirt lids. Squirt designs or pictures onto cardboard or heavy paper.

Good Soap Bubbles

1 cup water

2 Tbsp. liquid detergent

1 Tbsp. glycerine

1/2 tsp. sugar

Mix all ingredients.

Makes strong iridescent bubbles.

Finger Paints

- Thicken tempera paint with child-safe wallpaper paste or art paste.
- Color liquid laundry starch with food coloring or tempera paint.
- Combine non-mentholated shaving cream with a few drops of food coloring. Paint on washable surface, not on paper.
- Combine 1 cup flour
  1/2 cup water
  Mix until creamy. Color with food coloring or tempera.

Shaker Paint

DO NOT USE TEMPERA POWDER FOR SHAKER PAINT. INHALING POWDERED PAINT MAY HARM LUNGS.

THINGS TO USE:

- natural ground spices, such as cinnamon, cloves, curry, etc.
- cornmeal
- salt or sugar mixed with a few drops of food coloring
- white "Super Sand" mixed with a few drops of food coloring or a teaspoon or two of liquid tempera

Method: Put shaker paint into containers with holes in the top, such as spice shakers, salt shakers, or small yogurt containers with holes made in the lid. Have children "paint" on paper with liquid glue to make a design and shake the shaker paint onto the glue. Shake excess off paper and return to shaker.

A Note on Tempera Paint:

Mixing detergent with tempera to make cleaning clothes easier DOES NOT WORK, as commonly believed. (This changes the PH balance of the paint and actually makes it harder to wash out.)

To Remove Tempera Paint From Clothes:

1. Rinse in lukewarm water as soon as possible, continuing until water runs clear.
2. Wash the item as usual and hope for the best. (With the variety of manufactured fabrics there are no guarantees.)

Our Suggestion:

Always use paint aprons or paintshirts; men's shirts with sleeves cut off and buttoned on backwards provide excellent coverage and often absorb drips well.

Goop

2 cups salt
2/3 cup water
1 cup cornstarch
1/2 cup water

Mix salt and water together in a saucepan. Heat for 3 or 4 minutes, until salt is dissolved. Remove from heat. Mix cornstarch and water. Add to saucepan, stirring very quickly to mix. Stir 2 to 3 minutes until mixture thickens. Add food coloring if you wish. Store indefinitely in foil or plastic.

Ice Crystal Paint

2 Tbsp. liquid starch
2 Tbsp. water
1 tsp. white liquid tempera
1/2 cup salt

Mix all ingredients well. As paint dries, it will crystallize and sparkle.

Easter Egg Dye

1/2 cup water
1 Tbsp. vinegar
few drops food coloring

Mix in small containers, using several different colors. Using a spoon, dip eggs into color. The longer you leave them, the stronger the color will be. Lay on paper towels to dry.

Pliable Plasticene

Warm hard plasticene in a 250° oven for a few minutes. This makes it easier for small hands to work with.

Things To Do with Paint

These paint activities encourage creativity and a willingness to experiment. We recommend that you set up each activity for at least a week so that every child gets a chance to enjoy the experience.

At the Easel

- Paint to a variety of music, such as waltzes, marches, and lullabies. Try to find music that conveys different moods.
- Add varying amounts of white to one color to create a range of four or five pastels. Using the same color, add varying amounts of black to it to make a range of four or five shades.
- Place two primary colors and one empty container at each easel, with three brushes. Let the children mix a new color.
- Put the three primary colors, plus white and black, in each of five sections of a twelve-space muffin tin. Provide spoons, and let the children mix new colors before painting their pictures.
- Put two or more double-sided easels next to each other to do cooperative painting. Have the children start on their own sheets of paper. After a suitable length of time have the children move one place to the right. Repeat until the children are back at their own easels, and allow them time to finish the picture if they wish. This could be done to music, with the children stopping when the music stops, in the same fashion as musical chairs.
- Give the children different shapes of paper to paint on, such as circles, squares, triangles, rectangles, and ovals.
- Give the children a sheet of paper with a shape cut out of the center. The children then have to paint around the shaped hole.

Different Kinds of Paper

- For a different effect, have the children paint on foil, newsprint, recycled clear plastic bags, wallpaper, gift-wrap, and so on.

Textures and Smells

- Mix different items such as sand, salt, sugar, flour, shampoo, cinnamon, cloves, and glitter with your paint to create paint with a variety of textures and smells.

Painting Outdoors

- Paint your outside playground equipment and pavement with large brushes and water.
- Paint pictures on the snow with large brushes and thin tempera paint.
- Paint a snowperson or sculpture made by the children, as above.
- Attach a large sheet of brown craft paper to an outdoor fence, and have the children paint a large mural.
- Put a large sheet of brown craft paper on the ground outside. Pour different colors of paint onto several cookie sheets or trays, and have the children walk in the paint and then across the paper with bare feet.

Micro and Macro Painting

Let the children experience the difference between large and small by setting up the following two activities at the same time. Encourage children to move back and forth from one to the other.

Micro Painting

Break the bottom half of an egg carton in two to form palettes with six sections. Pour small amounts of different colors of paint into each section. Give the children cotton swabs and small pieces of paper. The children will paint tiny pictures.

Macro Painting

Put large pieces of brown craft paper on the floor. Provide the children with containers of paint large enough to handle 10- or 12-cm (4- or 5-inch) paint brushes. They will enjoy painting large pictures, and will probably move back and forth between the micro and macro painting several times. They may even change their voices to match the type of painting they are doing.

Different Tools

- To create a different effect, have the children paint with small paint rollers, feathers, toothbrushes, twigs, and so on.
- Paint with a straw used as a brush, or blow through the straw at thin paint dropped on the paper.

Paint on Things

- Paint on recycled boxes from cereal or other food, rocks the children have collected, or a piece of sanded wood.
- Paint on the windows. This washes off easily, and is nice to do on special occasions such as Valentine's Day or Christmas. (Add a little cornstarch to the paint first to make it stick.)
- Paint faces on paper bags (top of head at closed end of bag) to make simple puppets.
- Paint faces on paper bags (chin at closed end of bag), stuff with newspaper, and tie above forehead. Fringe paper at top for hair, and you have a simple sculpture.

Painting at a Table

- Sprinkle bits of crushed eggshell on the paper, and help children paint over this with a roller and tempera paint. When the paint is dry, pick off the bits of eggshell. You will have a snowfall effect.
- Give the children several lengths of string or wool to lay out on their papers. Paint with roller and tempera as above, then remove the string or wool.

Printing

Put a sponge soaked with paint in a shallow container and use various tools for printmaking.

- kitchen utensils, such as a potato masher, cookie cutters, jar lids, plastic inserts from spice jars (with holes), and so on
- various sand molds, alphabet-shaped molds
- rubber-tipped, unsharpened pencils make great snow or dots

Things To Do with Sand

Discover

- Have containers of different volumes for the children to use in the sandbox. Try to have some that are graduated in size, for example, cups, pints, and quarts.
- Provide containers of the same volume but different shapes.
- Put a balance scale in the sandbox. Let the children weigh dry, damp, and wet sand. Which is heavier? Why?
- Let the children fill several film canisters with sand and then use the canisters as weights on the balance scale.
- Purchase a good sand wheel to use in the sandbox.
- Provide funnels and plastic tubing (wide enough for dry sand to go through).
- Use wet sand to mold shapes with different-shaped containers. How many things can the children make?
- Sprout beans in sand from the sandbox. Make sure the sand is good and moist. Then put it in a dishpan or other good-sized container. Have the children push the beans into the sand with their fingers. Let the children observe how the seeds sprout and start to grow. This sand should be thrown out when you are finished. If you prefer to reuse the sand, be sure to sterilize it by heating it in a 350° oven for 30 minutes, stirring the sand often.
- Using different-sized sieves, see how many sizes of sand are in the sandbox. Pieces of screen with varying grades of mesh make good sifters. Be sure to cover the sharp edges of the screen with electrical tape.
- Add rice, tiny pebbles, unpopped corn, gravel, and so on, to the sand. Let the children sift the sand and classify the items they find. Then make a chart that shows what the children find in the sand.
- Use a magnifying glass to observe the sand up close. What do the children see?

Create and Play

- Use a large, shallow plastic bowl or container filled with water to create a lake in the sandbox. Then landscape the lake with small rocks.
- Provide—or help the children make—small boats to float on the lake. Add models of fish, frogs, lizards, and other freshwater creatures.
- Turn the lake into a farm pond. Put model farm animals in the sandbox around the pond, and float ducks on the water. Pine cones and small branches make nice "forests" around the lake.
- Place rubber or plastic insects instead of animals around the sandbox lake.

- Add medium-sized rocks and plastic dinosaur models to the lake to make a "dinoscape."
- Replace the water in the bowl with saltwater, turning the lake into an ocean. Put toy sea animals and creatures into the water. If you do not have plastic ones, let the children help make them out of polystyrene trays. Put seashells on the "beach" around the ocean.
- Use fingers, hands, and various objects to make "animal footprints" in the sand.
- Turn the sandbox into a construction site, with building equipment such as plastic blocks, wooden sticks, bits of wood, rocks, and so on.
- Make straight roads, winding roads, country roads, city roads, and highways in the sandbox. For buildings, use small boxes with windows and doors drawn on. Wooden blocks can be used, but make sure they are not left in the damp sand overnight.
- Using damp sand, make different earth formations. Make mountains, hills, deserts, canyons, and islands around the lake or ocean.
- Have the children wear hats and sunglasses and carry buckets and shovels. Pretend that you are at the beach. Set up a "picnic" blanket nearby .
- Use mixing bowls, spoons, and flour sifters to make sand pancakes or cakes. Sprinkle on dry sand for "sugar." If the sand used for the cakes is white, use colored sand for the sugar.

Pictures and Prints

- In wet sand, use a variety of tools to draw pictures.
- In dry sand, use plastic squirt bottles of water to make the pictures.
- In either wet or dry sand, make shapes, letters of the alphabet, or numbers .
- In wet sand, use any of the following objects to make prints: potato mashers, spoons, wooden sticks, sand molds, rulers, cookie cutters, or any plastic toys with textures or pictures that will print. (Some nesting toys have good textures or prints on the bottom.) Use hands, fingers, feet, or shapes from a shape sorter.
- Spread glue on paper, then sprinkle on sand to make a sand picture. If you have white sand, color a small amount with food coloring to make colorful sand pictures.
- Make sand prints. Use enough sand to cover a cookie sheet or other tray. Then create a design with glue on a piece of paper. Put the paper, glue side down, into the sand. Press gently all over with your hand to make a print. Older children will enjoy making letters and numbers.
- Use small stones, dried beans, pumpkin seeds, or rice to make patterns in the

sand. Use sifters to remove the objects from the sand when you are ready to create new patterns.

- Use combs to make patterns in the sand. Make your own sand combs by cutting patterns into the edges of heavy cardboard.

Treasure Hunts

- Hide different plastic shapes in the sand. Then have the children find the shapes by slowly and carefully running their hands through the sand. Make a chart of the various shapes the children find. This is fun for the children to do blindfolded, identifying the shapes by feel.
- Paint small stones "gold" and hide them in the sand. Then have the children hunt for gold.
- Hide safe, metal objects in the sand. Have children use magnets to find the objects.
- Ask the local butcher for several large soup bones. Boil the bones at home to clean off all of the meat. Then bury the bones in the sandbox, and let the children discover the "dinosaur" bones. This is fun in a large, outdoor sand pit.

Fun Things to Use

- bottles with holes in the lids to sprinkle water
- salt and paper shakers or spice jars to sprinkle dry sand
- cans with both ends cut out to make tunnels (Make sure there are no sharp edges.)
- PVC pipe (plastic pipe used in plumbing)
- cooking utensils and muffin tins
- spoons, as many different spoons as you can find—large, small, doll-size, spoons with holes, ladles, graduated measuring spoons, and so on

More Creative Ideas

- Make paper-tube sandcastles. Cut the paper tubes into various sizes, spread glue on the outside of the tubes, and roll them in dry sand. Cone-shaped paper cups make good turret roofs. Glue the pieces together to make castles. Polystyrene meat trays make sturdy bases to transport castles home.
- Make layered sand jars, using different textures and colors of sand. (Sand can be colored with food coloring.) Other materials can be layered with the sand, such as pebbles, rice, beans, and so on.

• Make "fossils" in your sandbox. Press insects, leaves, toy animals, or shells into wet sand to make the impressions. Mix plaster of Paris with water to a creamy but pourable consistency. Pour mixture into imprints, and let it harden overnight. Remove the fossils when the plaster of Paris is fully set.

Water Exploration

Indoor Discovery

Add soap and food coloring to the water in your water table. Using a variety of containers, mix, pour, and experiment with color combinations.

Use paintbrushes and water to paint on chalkboards. Watch your pictures dry. Do it again and try blowing on the pictures.

Float ice cubes in the water. Make special cubes out of colored water. Try to find a variety of small, medium, and large containers in which to freeze water. Ask children to determine which size melts first. Freeze small plastic animals, leaves, flower petals, etc. in the ice cubes. Freeze marbles in the ice cubes. Do they float the same way as cubes made from just water?

Place two plastic bowls, one full of water, and one empty, in an empty water table, or on a tray on top of a table. Using different types of sponges, transfer the water from one bowl to another.

To relieve the winter doldrums, set up an indoor wading pool. Put towels on the floor to catch drips, fill the pool just a little way with warm water, and have children wear their bathing suits for a winter beach party.

Outdoor Discovery

Use buckets of water and large paintbrushes to paint your outdoor equipment. Paint swings and slides, bicycles, and storage sheds. Paint pictures on the pavement, and watch them evaporate.

On a nice day, put everyone into bathing suits, and use a variety of "squirters," such as pumps, empty detergent bottles, and basters. Please do not use squirt guns. Agree on a rule that says, "You can only squirt people who want to be squirted."

Fill the pool, put out a sprinkler, or run a hose down the slide. Have a bike wash. Throw pebbles into the pool to observe the concentric circles.

Nature and Science

Collect some pond water to put on the science table. Try to get some interesting bugs, such as water striders, with the water. Observe with a magnifying glass. What can you see?

Talk about things that live in the water. Obtain and observe tadpoles, goldfish, or guppies in your classroom. What do they eat? Why must you change the water?

Discuss the difference between freshwater and saltwater. Can you observe some salt water creatures? Put out some books with pictures of lakes, rivers, oceans, and streams. Display pictures of animals in or near water.

Plants and trees need water, too. Bring in two identical small plants. Water one, but not the other, for a few days. What happens? Why? Do this only for a few days so that both plants have a chance to live.

Observe how water evaporates. Fill two jars halfway with water. Mark the level on the jars with an indelible marker. Put a lid on one, and leave the other uncovered. What happens? Try this with salty water. Taste the residue left in the jar. What is it?

Put some containers outside to catch and measure the rainfall. Use a coffee filter to filter the rainwater. Can you see any dirt particles?

Bring water to a boil in a kettle or pot. Hold a metal baking sheet over the vapor, and observe the water droplets forming and then falling. Discuss where water comes from, how clouds are formed, and the fact that we need to conserve water.

Water is in rain, snow, fog, and clouds. When we breathe out, we are forming miniclouds. Collect snow. Tell the children that snow is solid water. Let it melt in a jar. Put the water through a filter. Is your snow clean or dirty? Do the same with ice you have collected from outside.

Observe water displacement. Place a clear plastic jar half-full of water on a tray (to catch spillage). Put an elastic band around the jar at the water level. Gently drop stones or marbles into the jar. What happens to the water level?

Put two baby-food jars in the water table, one with the lid off and one with the lid on. What happens when you push on them? Why won't the capped jar stay under the water?

Put some sand in the jar with the lid on and replace the lid. Keep adding more until it sinks. Relate this to what happens in a submarine.

Rinse out baby-food jars and fill three with cold water, three with warm water. Put a teaspoon of sugar, salt, and soap into the three cold jars, respectively, and a teaspoon into the warm jars. Cap and shake the jars. Which ones dissolve faster?

Fill one jar with hot water, one with cold water. Let children feel the temperature of both. Pour the contents of both jars into a large jar. What happens to the temperature?

Using some clear plastic tubing and a bucket, set up a siphon from the water table to the bucket. Keeping the water flowing through the tubing into the bucket, lift the bucket to a table higher than the water level. What happens? This activity demonstrates that water naturally flows downhill.

Creative Play

Make a collage of the many different uses of water. Collages may contain pictures of gardens, toothbrushes, firetrucks, washing machines, showers, swimming pools, etc.

Wash dishes, clothes, and toys in the dramatic play center. Use soapy water and rags to wash the tables, shelves, and other equipment in the classroom.

Put rainy day dress-up clothes, boots, and umbrellas in the dramatic play center.

Bring in an inflatable boat. Pretend that you are boating, camping, fishing, etc. Make fishing poles with magnets and strings. Cut fish shapes out of paper, meat trays, or cardboard boxes. Attach paper clips to the shapes and go fishing with your magnet.

Make boats in the woodworking center. Make small boats out of half walnut shells, with a bit of plasticene in the bottom, a straw for a mast, and a paper sail. Use your breath for wind power. Tie two or three meat trays together with lengths of string to make barges. Place blocks, plastic play figures, pebbles, etc. on the barges. How much can they carry without going under?

Use food coloring, water, and plastic containers to mix colors. Use your colors to "paint" a picture. Dip white paper towels into the colored water and hang to dry. See what color combinations you end up with.

Draw a pastel picture, and then spray with water to get an unusual effect. Draw on wet paper with chalk. Dip your brush into dry tempera paint and paint on wet paper.

Tear up some crepe paper and place in a small container. Pour a little water into the container. What happens? Use this "crepe paper" paint to paint a picture. This is also good for dying Easter eggs since the colors are so rich.

Fun things to Use with Water

PVC pipe. Hose. Plastic tubing. Straws. Basters. Eye and medicine droppers. Funnels. Ladles. Eggbeaters. Were whips. Spoons. Measuring spoons. Measuring cups. Graduated volume containers. Squirt bottles. Soap. Shaving cream. Sieves. Empty film canisters. Shells. Plastic fish and creatures. Boats.

Neighborhood Outings

The community surrounding your school is a rich resource for your program. Neighborhood walks and visits can be a regular part of your routine. Neighborhood outings have many advantages:

- Destinations are easily reached on foot.
- Planning can be spontaneous.
- Outings provide opportunities for family involvement.
- Outings can enhance specific aspects of your program or simply provide an opportunity "to get away from it all".
- Children learn about the community and the community gets involved in your program.

Obtaining Permission

Whether or not your regulations require that permission be obtained before taking children off the school premises, it is in your best interest to get consent before leaving school. The permission forms at the end of this section can be used to ensure that consent has been secured. Each form serves a different function:

Notice of Field Trip: If you have a bit of time to plan your outing, send this form home for a signature several days in advance of venturing out.

Spontaneous Trip Form: This blanket permission form, signed by parents or guardians at registration, will allow for spontaneous neighborhood outings.

Field Trips: For programs that do not have blanket permission forms, this form is posted in a common area; it describes your outing and asks for each guardian's signature at school when dropping off children, usually on the morning of your outing. Be sure to draw guardians' attention to the form on the day of the outing.

As long as there are enough staff and volunteers to accompany you on your outing, one staff member will have to stay behind with those children not able to go. If there are not enough adults to go around, it may be necessary to abandon your plans.

Where to Go

Although the possibilities for destinations are only limited by your imagination, here are some that have worked for us:

The Bank   The Junk Dealer

The Barber Shop   The Laundromat

The Book Store   The Pharmacy

The Farmers' Market	The Pizza Shop
The Fire Station	The Post Office
The Florist	The Sporting Goods Store
The Grocery Store	The Toy Store
The Hair Stylist	A Well-Protected Construction Site

Some places are more suited to large groups than others; you will have to use your judgement. If a small group is a better idea, you may wish to take a few students at a time, or split the class to simultaneously visit a variety of destinations. Again, use your judgement; the children may also be able to help you with that decision.

When to Go
- when it is time to supplement some aspect of your program
- when you need to make a purchase
- when it is time to broaden children's horizons
- when children's behavior requires a change of atmosphere or extended exercise
- just for a change of pace
- just for fun

Preparation
1. Preparation for children
   - Safety and Etiquette — While it is necessary to review the guidelines below just prior to your departure, they should be second nature to the children as a regular part of your behavior expectations. The underlying theme is respect for oneself and respect for others.
   - About the destination — Talk about where you are going and the things children can expect to see there. Prepare your group to look out for anything special that you may be using or talking about in your program once you return. Familiarize children with the names of people they may meet. Build a sense of expectation and adventure about your walk, your final destination, and any follow-up activities you will do upon your return. Remind children of things they may see along the way that they have seen before.
2. Preparation for teachers
   - Establish a strong rapport with community members well in advance of your outings by shopping in local businesses, getting to know managers and proprietors, and ensuring that they are aware of your presence in the community.

- Phone ahead to inform shopkeepers about your visit.
- Determine in advance the group's ability to cope with the circumstances of your outing. It's best to plan a very short trip at first. Expect to develop over a period of time the children's ability to behave well while out in the community.
- Review guidelines below just before leaving school.
- Ensure that you have permission from every family.
- Post a sign in the morning informing families of the details of your trip.
- Post a note on your door indicating where you have gone.
- Choose some songs to sing along the way and on your return. Take a familiar tune and change the words to suit the experience.

Guidelines for Children

3 Easy-to-Remember Safety Rules:

1. Always listen for your teacher's voice.
2. Always stay with the group.
3. Keep your eyes ahead and feet walking.

3 Easy-to-Remember Rules of Etiquette:

1. Always use gentle words and voices.
2. Touch only when you're invited to touch.
3. When someone is talking, it's time to listen.

Guidelines for Staff

- Ensure that you have adequate supervision: Never have fewer than two adults on any outing. Invite volunteers to join you (see Volunteer Form).

- Bring a backpack (it allows you to have two free hands) with a first aid kit and emergency phone numbers (see Personal Information Form).

- Along the way, place staff in strategic positions:
  1. Head of group — makes sure it is safe to cross streets, alerts other adults to hazards
  2. Middle of group — supervises group in front of her or him
  3. Rear of group — watches group in front of him or her, ensures slow walkers stay with group.

- Remember to have follow-up activities after you've returned to reinforce the experience for the children. Stories, storytelling, dramatic play, crafts, games, and songs all make your outing more meaningful and lasting for the children.

- An outing is an adventure! Although children must be mindful of safety and etiquette, ensure that they also ask questions, make comments, and have fun!

Notice of Field Trip

Dear Family:

Our group is planning a field trip outside of school. Please read the information below. Then detach and return the Permission Slip as soon as possible.

Date _____ Destination _____

Departure Time _____ Return Time _____

Accompanying Staff/Volunteers _____

Method of Transportation _____

Cost _____ Items to Send _____

Additional Information _____

_____

- -

Permission Slip

My child _____ has permission to attend

the field trip to _____

I am available to help out   Yes ____ No ____

_____   _____
date   parent or guardian signature

Spontaneous Trip Form

Form II

Dear Family:

Occasionally we go on walks in the neighborhood, especially in fine weather. Since this requires spontaneous planning, we request that you provide blanket permission for such outings by signing below.

I permit _____ to go on impromptu neighborhood walks with the group.

Signature _____ Date _____

I wish to be informed prior to every walking trip taken by the school.

Signature _____ Date _____

- -

Form III

Date _____

Dear Family:

Today/Tomorrow we will be walking to _____

Please sign below to indicate that you are aware of our plans.

CHILD'S NAME _____

PARENT OR GUARDIAN SIGNATURE _____

Thanks for your cooperation.

Field Trips

Destination _____ Costs _____

Address _____

Trip Date _____ Date Confirmed _____

Contact Person _____ Phone _____

_____

Route _____

Group _____ No. of Children _____

Staff _____

Volunteers _____

Departure Time _____ Return Time _____

Notes _____

_____

Evaluation _____

_____

Classroom Activities

Pretrip	Follow-up	Songs/Stories

Personal Information

Emergency Phone _____   Center Phone _____

Child/Health Insurance	Mother	Father	Alternate
	Home: Work:	Home: Work:	Home: Work:
	Home: Work:	Home: Work:	Home: Work:
	Home: Work:	Home: Work:	Home: Work:
	Home: Work:	Home: Work:	Home: Work:
	Home: Work:	Home: Work:	Home: Work:
	Home: Work:	Home: Work:	Home: Work:
	Home: Work:	Home: Work:	Home: Work:
	Home: Work:	Home: Work:	Home: Work:
	Home: Work:	Home: Work:	Home: Work:

Song List

Action Songs

1. I'm a Little Teapot
2. Pop Goes the Weasel
3. Row Row Row Your Boat
4. Teddy Bear, Teddy Bear
5. The Wheels on the Bus
6. _____
7. _____
8. _____
9. _____
10. _____

Counting Songs

1. Five in a Bed
2. Five Little Monkeys
3. Five Little Speckled Frogs
4. One Elephant, Two Elephants
5. This Old Man
6. _____
7. _____
8. _____
9. _____
10. _____

Animal Songs

1. B.I.N.G.O.
2. Eensy Weensy Spider
3. How Much Is that Doggy
4. Little Arabella Miller
5. Old MacDonald
6. _____
7. _____
8. _____
9. _____
10. _____

Feelings

1. Ally Bally
2. If You're Happy and You Know It
3. Hello Everybody
4. Lazy Mary
5. Warm Kitty
6. _____
7. _____
8. _____
9. _____
10. _____

Circle Games

1. Farmer in the Dell
2. Hokey Pokey
3. London Bridge
4. Looby Loo
5. Ring Around the Rosie
6. _____
7. _____
8. _____
9. _____
10. _____

Folk Songs

1. Kookaburra
2. Kum-Ba-Ya
3. Michael Row Your Boat
4. Swing Low Sweet Chariot
5. When the Saints
6. _____
7. _____
8. _____
9. _____
10. _____

Multicultural Songs

1. My Little Farm (Hispanic)
2. Alouette (French)
3. Head, Shoulders, Baby (African-American)
4. Frère Jacques (French)
5. A Ram Sam Sam (African)
6. _____
7. _____
8. _____
9. _____
10. _____

Seasons and Weather

1. Come Let Us Pull, Pull, Pull
2. Daffodil, Daffodil
3. The More It Snows
4. Rain Is Falling Down
5. Shake, Shake the Apple Tree
6. _____
7. _____
8. _____
9. _____
10. _____

My Body

1. Can You Walk on Two Legs
2. Head and Shoulders
3. Put Your Finger in the Air
4. This Is the Way We Wash Our Hands
5. Where is Thumbkin
6. _____
7. _____
8. _____
9. _____
10. _____

Others

_____
_____
_____
_____
_____
_____
_____
_____

Nursery Rhymes

1. Baa Baa Black Sheep
2. Hickory Dickory Dock
3. Humpty Dumpty
4. Old King Cole
5. Three Blind Mice
6. _____
7. _____
8. _____
9. _____
10. _____

 # Phone Numbers

Staff

Name	Address	Phone

General

Name	Address	Phone

 # Emergency Numbers

Police _____

Fire _____

Ambulance _____

Poison _____

Electricity _____

Heating _____

Garbage Disposal _____

Cleaning Services _____

Food Services _____

Custodian _____

_____   _____

_____   _____

_____   _____

_____   _____

_____   _____

_____   _____

Accident Report

Child's Name _____ Date _____

Injury _____ Date/Time of injury _____

Where accident occurred _____

Staff supervising area where accident occurred _____

Staff located near area where accident occurred _____

Staff on duty at time of injury _____

Witnesses to accident _____

Details of accident _____

_____

_____

Action taken _____

_____

Suggestions for prevention_____

_____

_____   Family Informed: Yes _____
        Staff Signature

                                    How: Phone/In Person

_____   When _____
        Head Teacher

                                    Family Comments _____

_____
        Assistant Director
                                    _____

_____
        Director

Substitute Teachers

Name	Phone	Days Available	Training

 # Resource People

Name	Specialty	Address	Phone

 # Class List

Name _____   Name _____

Guardian _____   Guardian _____

Address _____   Address _____

Phone _____   Phone _____
　　　　Home　　　　Bus.　　　　　　　　　　　　Home　　　　Bus.

Emerg. Ph. _____   Emerg. Ph. _____

Reminders _____

Name _____   Name _____

Guardian _____   Guardian _____

Address _____   Address _____

Phone _____   Phone _____
　　　　Home　　　　Bus.　　　　　　　　　　　　Home　　　　Bus.

Emerg. Ph. _____   Emerg. Ph. _____

Reminders _____

Name _____   Name _____

Guardian _____   Guardian _____

Address _____   Address _____

Phone _____   Phone _____
　　　　Home　　　　Bus.　　　　　　　　　　　　Home　　　　Bus.

Emerg. Ph. _____   Emerg. Ph. _____

Reminders _____

Name _____   Name _____

Guardian _____   Guardian _____

Address _____   Address _____

Phone _____   Phone _____
　　　　Home　　　　Bus.　　　　　　　　　　　　Home　　　　Bus.

Emerg. Ph. _____   Emerg. Ph. _____

Reminders _____

Attendance

Group _____ Month _____ Week _____

Name	Monday in	Monday out	Tuesday in	Tuesday out	Wednesday in	Wednesday out	Thursday in	Thursday out	Friday in	Friday out
Total										

 # Shopping List

Number	Item	Supplier

Inventory List

Science ☐   Sensory ☐   Table-Top Toys ☐

Puzzles ☐   Cognitive ☐   Gross-Motor ☐

Floor Toys ☐   Drama ☐   Creative ☐

_____ ☐   _____ ☐   _____ ☐

No.	Item	Complete	Repair/ Paint	Replace	OK

 # Allergies

Child	Allergy	Precautions

Health Notes

Child	Medical Information

Meeting Notes

Date _____ Topic _____

_____
_____
_____
_____
_____
_____
_____
_____
_____
_____
_____
_____
_____
_____
_____
_____
_____
_____

Things to Do _____

_____
_____
_____
_____
_____

Menu

Week _____ Theme _____

S N A C K	MONDAY	TUESDAY	WEDNESDAY	THURSDAY	FRIDAY	
						a.m.
L U N C H						
S N A C K						p.m.

Reminders _____

S N A C K	MONDAY	TUESDAY	WEDNESDAY	THURSDAY	FRIDAY	
						a.m.
L U N C H						
S N A C K						p.m.

Reminders _____

Themes: Ideas and Notes

Topic	Content

Fire Drill Procedure

Primary Exit _____

_____

Secondary Exit _____

_____

Our Emergency Shelter is _____

_____

_____

Draw your escape plan below.

Fire Drill Procedure

General Information

When the alarm sounds KEEP CALM.

All adults: Gather all of the children and line them up at the door. COUNT THEM.

First adult: Take attendance book and start leaving with the children.

Second adult: Check all playrooms, storage areas, and bathrooms to be sure no children are left behind.

Last adult: Switch off lights. Make sure that all children are departing ahead of you. Leave the room last and close the doors.

Primary Exit _____

Secondary Exit _____

Evacuation Procedure

_____
_____
_____
_____
_____
_____
_____
_____
_____
_____
_____
_____
_____
_____

TEACHERS OUTSIDE:

If any groups are slow in evacuating, one or two teachers should return to the exit(s) to assist.

STAY IN GROUPS UNTIL THE ALL-CLEAR SIGNAL IS GIVEN.

ALWAYS KNOW HOW MANY CHILDREN ARE PRESENT IN YOUR GROUP.

OUR EMERGENCY SHELTER IS _____

 # Birthdays

Staff

January	July
_____ _____	_____ _____
_____ _____	_____ _____
_____ _____	_____ _____

February	August
_____ _____	_____ _____
_____ _____	_____ _____
_____ _____	_____ _____

March	September
_____ _____	_____ _____
_____ _____	_____ _____
_____ _____	_____ _____

April	October
_____ _____	_____ _____
_____ _____	_____ _____
_____ _____	_____ _____

May	November
_____ _____	_____ _____
_____ _____	_____ _____
_____ _____	_____ _____

June	December
_____ _____	_____ _____
_____ _____	_____ _____
_____ _____	_____ _____

Birthdays

Children

January	July
February	August
March	September
April	October
May	November
June	December

Festival of Saint Anthony the Abbot, Mexico

On January 17, the children of Mexico commemorate Saint Anthony the Abbot, who loved both children and animals. The children wash and brush their pets and put hats and decorated collars on them. Then they all join in a parade, taking the animals to church to be blessed. The pets include everything from dogs and cats to goats and goldfish.

This is a good time to talk to the children about pets and other animals. Discuss the fact that many animals rely on human beings to take care of them, and that we should treat the animals with respect. Tell the children about the Humane Society and the role of that organization in caring for animals.

Activities

- Ask someone from the Humane Society or a local pet store to visit the classroom to talk about animals. If possible, ask the visitor to bring along an appropriate pet for the children to meet.

- Have the children bring their favorite stuffed animals to school. Then let the children make fancy collars for the animals to wear. Make "serapes" for the children out of brown craft paper, brightly colored with crayons or marking pens. Have the children put on the serapes and tie them in place with string around the waist, and have a "parade of the animals" with the children playing on maracas, drums, and flutes or recorders as they march around.

- In the dramatic play area of your classroom, set up a "market" with small tables, "pesos" made of yellow circles of construction paper, and baskets for the shoppers. Typical items in your market could be vegetables, fruits, toys, clothes, and snacks. (Corn chips would be appropriate.) Play lively Mexican music for background. Let the children wear their serapes, and if possible provide straw hats for them to wear. Tell the children that in many countries, the day-to-day shopping is done in outdoor markets rather than in large supermarkets or shopping malls.

- Serve typical Mexican snacks at snack time, for example, tortillas or corn chips with refried beans. Two popular drinks in Mexico are hot chocolate with a touch of cinnamon, and liquado, a drink made of ripe bananas, strawberries, chunks of pineapple, and fresh orange juice blended together.

January Activities

Song • January Song •

(Tune of Frère Jacques)

Chill wind's blowing, chill wind's blowing,
(Hug self)
On my cheeks, on my nose.
(Touch cheeks/nose)
Wrap my scarf around me, make it all surround me,
(Pretend to wrap scarf around neck several times)
Keeps me snug, keeps me warm.
(Hug self again)

Flakes are floating, flakes are drifting,
(Flutter fingers downwards)
Gently down, all around.
(Flutter fingers all around)
Landing on my lashes, and on men's moustaches.
(Touch eye/make a moustache with index finger)
Silv'ry coat, on the ground.
(Move hands, fingers spread, as if gently rubbing the ground)

Circle Activity • Winter Birds •

The white blanket outdoors provides a great contrast to the bright colors of winter birds. If you have birdfeeders set up outside, birds will be flocking to your windows. This activity will help children identify visiting birds.

1. Borrow a variety of pictures of winter birds from your public library or local school library. Spend time with your group discussing the unique features of each winter bird.

2. After several days of reviewing the pictures with your group, play a guessing game. Turn over all the pictures. A child chooses a picture and describes several features of that bird to the group. Invite the children to guess which winter bird is being described. Once all pictures have been described, leave them at an activity table for the children to play with in small groups. Older groups can also use word cards to match with the pictures.

Snack • Simple Rice Pudding •

(Pongal—Southern India)

During this festival, people in Southern India honor the sun's contribution to the rice crops. Rice is cooked in milk, offered to the Sun God, Surya, and then tasted by the celebrants.

Bring cooked rice, brown or white, for your group, or cook it at school. Pour some warm milk over the warmed rice, and sprinkle with a bit of sugar, honey, or maple syrup. Enjoy as a snack or dessert after lunch.

Table Activity • Snowflake Match-up •

You'll need:

- white paper cut into 5 x 5" squares
- black construction paper cut into 5 x 5" squares
- glue
- scissors

1. Cut white paper into pairs of snowflakes and mount the paper snowflakes on the black squares. More intricate snowflake designs will suit older age groups.
2. Place the snowflake cards on a table and have children match pairs.

VARIATIONS:

1. Cut more than two of each snowflake shape.
2. Children can turn all cards face down, then turn up one at a time trying to match pairs.

Circle Game • Winter Dressup •

You'll need:

- Bristol board in a variety of colors
- fabric hook-and-loop fastener in strips (available in sewing departments)
- snowperson's hat, scarf, mittens, boots, and buttons cut out of Bristol board, with small fabric hook-and-loop fastener pieces attached to back
- large snowperson mounted on Bristol board with fabric hook-and-loop fastener pieces where appropriate clothing items should go

1. Place clothing cutouts in a bag.
2. The first child chooses an item from the bag.
3. The group sings "January Song" while the child attaches the clothing item to the appropriate place on the snowperson.
4. The first child then holds the bag while a friend in the circle chooses the next item.
5. Continue until every child has had a turn.

Recipe • Fruity Snowballs •

You'll need:

- 8 ounces cream cheese
- 1 Tbsp. honey
- 1/4 cup raisins, chopped
- 1/4 cup nuts, chopped
- 1/8 tsp. each nutmeg and cinnamon
- 1/4 cup shredded coconut

1. Blend cream cheese and honey with fork.
2. Mix in raisins, nuts, and spices, one at a time.
3. Roll into small balls.
4. Roll balls in coconut.
5. Snowballs can be eaten at room temperature or chilled.

Group Activity • Winter Garden •

Turn winter white to green by planting an herb garden. Before you begin, have a sunny spot ready in which to place your pots.

You'll need:

- 4" pots
- potting soil
- herb seeds suited to pot culture: sage, basil, parsley, marjoram, savory, thyme
- newspaper
- spoons
- water
- wooden sticks or tongue depressors

1. Set up a workstation with all stages of the activity laid out in order.
2. Children start their own plants by spooning soil into an individual pot, watering soil well, and pressing seeds gently into soil. Avoid overseeding.
3. Mark children's names and herb names on wooden sticks and place in pots.
4. Place pots on a cookie sheet in a sunny spot.
5. Tend regularly, but do not overwater.
6. When plants have grown, arrange a group taste test.
7. Try adding your herbs as an ingredient in recipes or meals; e.g., dill and parsley are delicious in egg salad, try basil in a vegetable soup.
8. Plants can be put into the garden in spring for continued use all summer. Some may even seed themselves and return next spring.

Hint: Keep plants well pinched back to maintain bushiness.

Craft • Ice-Crystal Pictures •

You'll need:

- 1/8 cup liquid starch
- 1/8 cup water
- 1 tsp. white tempera
- 1/2 cup table salt
- shirt cardboard

1. Mix all ingredients together.
2. Paint a picture on the shiny side of shirt cardboard.
3. As the paint mixture dries, it will crystallize.

February Special Event

Chinese New Year, China

The most important Chinese holiday, New Year, requires a great deal of preparation. People settle arguments so that they can start the new year with a clean slate. They scrub and decorate their homes, using red as much as possible because red is the color of celebration and good luck. Red and pink flowers are distributed throughout the house, and red scrolls with the symbols for Gung Hay Fat Choy are hung by the door. Gung Hay Fat Choy means "wishing you prosperity" or "Happy New Year." Gifts of money or other small tokens are wrapped in red paper and given by older relatives to young children. The gifts, meant as tokens of celebration and good luck, are called Lai See.

The climax of the five-day holiday is the parade led by the Dragon, which represents goodness, strength, and hope for the future. Its face is made to look fierce in order to scare the evil spirits away and to ensure a good year.

Activities

- Make Lai See. Tape a few pennies into the center of a piece of red paper, and fold it into a small parcel. Teach the children the phrase Gung Hay Fat Choy. Then have the children take turns presenting each other with Lai See and wishing each other Happy New Year.

- Fireworks are a big part of the Chinese New Year celebration. Have the children use black paper, brightly colored paints, and straws to make straw paintings. (See "Things To Do with Paint.") The results look like fireworks in the sky!

- Decorate the classroom. Hang red streamers from the ceiling, and glue bits of pink and white tissue paper to a few small bare branches for cherry blossoms.

- Make red scrolls to hang near the doorways. Print the words Gung Hay Fat Choy on pieces of red construction paper. Have the children decorate the scrolls with glitter, bits of foil, and so on. To hang the scrolls, tape drinking straws horizontally to the backs and thread a string through.

- Have the children make paper-bag dragons. Use marking pens, brightly colored paper, cloth, and so on, to decorate brown paper bags. Attach long streamers to the bottom of the bags. Then have a dragon parade with drums and cymbals. You can also make a large classroom dragon and let the children take turns being the dragon. Tell the children that the dragon moves in and out through the parade, rather than walking at the beginning of the parade.

February Activities

Song • Did You Ever See Some Snowflakes? •

(Tune of "Did You Ever See a Lassie?")

The children contribute their own winter images to this song.
Here are several suggestions to start them off:

Did you ever see some snowflakes, some snowflakes, some snowflakes?
Did you ever see some snowflakes fluttering down?

Did you ever see a snowman, a snowman, a snowman?
Did you ever see a snowman on a cold winter day?

Did you ever see an icicle, an icicle, an icicle?
Did you ever see an icicle sparkling in the sun?

Did you ever see a skier, a skier, a skier?
Did you ever see a skier whizzing down a hill?

Did you ever see some children, some children, some children?
Did you ever see some children playing in the snow?

Circle Game • Winter Things •

1. Collect several "winter things" such as a scarf, a glove, a ski, a sliding toy.
2. Start a discussion by saying, "We all know what these things are usually used for" and talk about their familiar uses.
3. Next, take each item and have the children suggest what else it might be used for. Remind them that this is an imagination game; any suggestion is acceptable.
4. Once each child has suggested a use for an item, go on to the next item.

Outdoor Activity • Experiments with Snow •

These activities will allow children an opportunity to discover the various properties of snow.

You'll need:

- sand buckets
- large spoons
- water in buckets
- food/yogurt containers

1. Place some snow in containers to bring inside. Observe how long it takes to melt. Is the remaining water clean or dirty?

2. Make a thick slush by adding a small amount of water to containers of snow. Find a spot in the yard to build a "slush castle." Check the condition of your castle the next day.

3. Use snowballs to draw pictures on outside walls of your building (an opportunity for the children to write on walls without ruffling any adult feathers).

4. Find a spot in the yard that is piled high with snow, and, using large kitchen spoons, dig out holes that could be burrows for animals to hide in.

5. Using containers and sand buckets, build snowcastles.

Snack • Groundhog Grog •

Since groundhogs are strictly vegetarian, celebrate their special day with a vegetable snack. Serve vegetable juice to drink, and crunchy vegetables to eat. (If serving carrots, have the children chew them well, or serve them grated, in paper cups.)

For a dip, mix dried or fresh parsley and dill weed into some sour cream or plain yogurt.

Movement Activity • Ice Sculptures •

Make sure there is lots of space to move around for this activity.

You'll need:

- tape recorder or record player
- different kinds of music for the children to move to (This is a perfect opportunity to use classical music to evoke different types of movements.)
- winter scarves or hats

1. Choose a cold day to talk to the children about cold winter weather.
2. Say, "Today we are so cold that we have turned into ice sculptures." Have the children put on hats, short scarves, or mitts.
3. Say, "Freeze your body into any shape."
4. Instruct children: "When I play the music, defrost and move around, or melt into a heap. When the music stops, freeze your body into another shape."
5. Have children freeze into high/low, wide/narrow, curved/straight, and animal shapes. Suggest that they listen carefully to the music so they will know how to move. Draw their attention to the varying moods of heavy/light, fast/slow, quiet/loud music.

Song • Glove Song •

(Tune of "Ten Little Indians")

Action: Hold fingers upward. Pretend to push each finger of "glove" onto fingers of other hand.

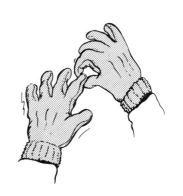

One little, two little, three little fingers,
Four little, five little, six little fingers,
Seven little, eight little, nine little fingers,
Ten fingers, now my gloves are on.
(Repeat action taking gloves "off" finger by finger.)

Creative Activity • Heartprints •

You'll need:

- heart-shaped doilies
- red, pink, and purple paints
- small sponge pieces, dampened
- clothespins
- plastic containers
- construction paper

1. Attach clothespins to sponge pieces.
2. Prepare containers with small amounts of paint in each and place sponges in containers.
3. Children place a doily on the paper and, holding onto the clothespin, dab over the doily with a sponge.
4. Doilies can be moved to different spots on paper and dabbed over with different colors of paint.

Group Activity • Ident-a-fruit •

Ask your grocery store's produce manager for fruit pictures that are often included with shipments.

1. Bring in a variety of exotic fruits, such as kiwi, mango, star fruit, ugli fruit, prickly pear, and papaya. Place the fruits together in a basket.
2. Use a map to show where the fruits were grown.
3. Pass each fruit around the circle, encouraging the children to (gently) feel and talk about the smells, shapes, sizes, and colors.
4. Play a matching game by setting up a table with your basket of fruit and matching picture cards (clipped from magazines or grocery fliers). Ask children to match the fruits with their respective pictures.
5. Later in the week, cut open the fruits one at a time. Note the difference between a vertical and horizontal cut. Pass each cut fruit

around in a small bowl for observation. Provide a table activity in which the children can match the fruit with its picture card.
6. Together make a fruit salad. Be sure to keep the peels for your compost pile.

International Earth Day

Earth Day is a good time to learn about our planet and the people who inhabit it. Preschool children are not too young to learn about Earth as part of a vast solar system, the makeup of the Earth, and the hunger, poverty, disease, and war that affect people in many parts of the world.

Activities

- Put up posters or mobiles of the solar system. Have available picture books that show the planet Earth and other planets in the solar system. Include pictures of the Milky Way.

- Make a galaxy mural. Do marble painting on various sizes and colors of construction paper circles (about 6" to 12"). When the paint is dry, mount the circles on black mural paper, spreading them out to form a solar system. Glue silver stars or glitter to the black paper.

- Make an Earth mural. Use paper and paint, magazine pictures, and so on, to illustrate the various features of the planet Earth. Include hills, mountains, prairies, plains, deserts, oceans, lakes, rivers, jungles, and forests.

- Make an inhabitants mural. Focus on the fact that all living things are inhabitants of the Earth. Use pictures of people of all races, animals, birds, sea life, insects, plants, and trees. Talk about how all of the creatures on Earth are interdependent.

- Find a way for the children in your school to help others in need. Some suggestions are: collect food for a food bank; bring in discarded toys that are still in good condition; make pictures to decorate an elderly care facility; take part in the Muscular Dystrophy Hop-a-thon, designed specifically for preschoolers; collect coins in a jar to contribute to an organization that helps relieve world hunger.

March Activities

Song • Five Birdie Friends •

(Tune of "Six Little Ducks")

Five birdies lived in my red maple tree.
(Hold up five fingers)
Flew down south to the sand and the sea.
(Flap "wings")
They spent their days keeping warm in the sun.
(Spread out arms, palms up, look upward
towards "sun," close eyes)
Waiting patiently 'til winter was done.
(Arms crossed, resting on chest)

March settled in with a warm gentle breeze.
(Hands in front, making a gentle waving motion)
Buds started showing on branches of trees.
(Arms up, hands in fists, fingers slowly opening)
Kids played outdoors from the morning 'til dark.
(Pretend to skip rope)
Families began to take long walks in the park.
(Make fingers walk)

Word spread down south that spring-things had begun.
(Hands cupped around mouth)
Birds headed home to get nest-building done.
(Spread arms and move "wings")
Soon from my tree I heard singing all day.
(Cup hand around one ear, then the other)
I knew 'til the fall my birdie friends planned to stay.
(Nod head)

Creative Activity • Wax Resist Easter Eggs •

You'll need:

- enough hard-boiled eggs for your group
- crayons
- crepe-paper dye (recipe below)
- spoons
- Easter grass/tissue paper
- egg carton/paper cup

1. Have children draw crayon designs on the hard-boiled eggs. Tell them to press firmly to ensure that the pictures will show up through the dye.
2. Dip eggs in a COOL dye bath. (Crepe-paper dye is made by placing strips of crepe paper into 1/2 cup hot water. Remove paper from solution and add 1 Tbsp. of vinegar to mixture. Let cool before using.)
3. Blot eggs on folded paper towels after each color dip.
4. Children can take their Easter eggs home in an egg carton section (use top and bottom taped together) or a small paper cup filled with Easter grass or colored tissue.
5. Blotter papers can be unfolded and used as placemats for snack or lunch.

Poem • Spring Has Sprung •

Spring has sprung, hoorah, hooray!
It's going to be a happy day.
With buzzing bees,
And leafy trees,
And flowers swaying in the breeze.

Food Activity • Maple-y Oatcakes •

You'll need:

- enough cooked oatmeal for your group; stir in a tablespoon or two of maple syrup during cooking.
- butter or margarine
- maple syrup
- large spoon or spatula

- electric frying pan
- individual small tin pie plates
- permanent marker for marking names on tin plates
- cookie sheet

1. Discuss safety rules for using frying pan.
2. Set pan temperature at medium-low to heat. Melt butter in pan.
3. Each child drops a large spoonful of thick porridge into the sizzling butter and presses it gently into pancake shape. Cook slowly.
4. Make sure edges are crispy brown before flipping.
5. Place finished oatcake in a tin plate; keep warm in oven until everyone is done.
6. Warm maple syrup before pouring over oatcakes.

Outdoor Activity • Muddy Fun •

After a rainy day, find a muddy spot in the corner of your yard, dress up in boots and raingear, and venture out to discover the pleasures of mud. Bring along a small bucket and spoon.

1. Just step around in the mud, and feel it squishing under your boots. Make muddy bootprints on the sidewalk.

2. Pick up a stick and draw in the mud.
3. Place some mud on nearby pavement and use your stick to make more drawings. (The next rain will wash it away.)
4. Collect mud in your bucket and make fingerpaintings and hand prints on fingerpaint paper back at school.
5. Using a stick, make pathways for streams of water in the mud.
6. Put some mud into the class water table in place of water.

Group Activity • Springtime Sprouts •

As outdoor plants and trees begin to sprout leaves, grow your own edible sprouts to put in sandwiches and salads. Have children observe the parts of the sprouts that look like all other plants. Start this activity on a Monday.

You'll need:

- small baby-food jars
- alfalfa seeds (from a health food store), rinsed
- cheesecloth, cut into 4" squares
- rubber bands
- large mixing bowl
- dish towel

1. Each child places 1 tsp. of seeds into jar and fills it with water, places cheesecloth over jar, and fixes it in place with rubber band.
2. Let seeds soak overnight.
3. Pour out water in the morning; rinse seeds in warm water and drain.
4. Repeat rinsing and draining twice a day without fail. (The children can do it in the morning, and you can do it in the afternoon.)
5. Drain very well to prevent seeds from sitting in water and rotting.
6. Keep in dark location.
7. Sprouts are ready when tails are 1–2" long (after about 3–5 days).

Creative Activity • Wind Chimes •

You'll need:

- enough tin plates for your group plus several extra
- found materials for gluing (e.g., fabric, paper, yarn scraps, buttons, drinking-straw pieces)
- white glue
- lengths of yarn or string

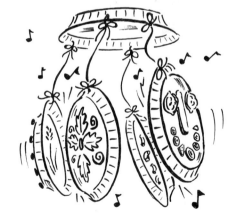

1. Prepare several tin plates in advance with holes around edge, lengths of yarn tied into the holes; set aside for use later.
2. Children decorate their own tin plates by gluing found materials onto both sides. (Names can be written with permanent marker.)
3. When glue is dry, attach children's plates to yarn lengths making sure that there is a noticeable "tinkling" sound when the plates hit each other.
4. Place assembled wind chimes in an outside doorway or window so that children can hear sound when wind blows.

April Special Event

International Children's Book Day

April 2, the birthday of Hans Christian Andersen, is celebrated as International Children's Book Day. It was established by the International Board on Books for Young People.

Activities

- Take a trip to your local library. Arrange in advance with the Children's Librarian to read several Hans Christian Andersen stories suitable for your group. Borrow these books from the library, and read them again throughout the week. If a trip to the library is too difficult to arrange, ask the librarian to come to the school.

- Have the children choose their favorite books from the class or school library. Let the children take the books home overnight for a family member to read as a bedtime story. Use chart paper to keep a record of the books that the children have borrowed.

- As a group, discuss the children's favorite books. First, tell the children about one of your favorites. Then invite the children to share their favorite books, either from school or from home.

- Create a group story, using chart paper, on any topic the children choose. Be sure to discuss "sequence of events"— that events in a story happen in a special order. This would also be a good time to introduce ordinal numbers—first, second, third, and so on. Use one piece of chart paper for each idea in your story. The children can then illustrate each page. Staple the pages together into a book, and work as a group to make a cover for it. Read the children's book to them at circle time.

- Put out special "book-writing paper" for the children to make and illustrate their own books. Let them dictate the stories as you print the words for them. They can then design a cover, while you print on the title, author, and illustrator. Encourage the children to share their stories with each other.

- Start a picture dictionary. In a blank workbook or scrapbook, print each letter of the alphabet at the top left of a double page. Provide magazines and catalogs. Let the children cut out pictures and glue them onto the appropriate pages. As you work with the children, emphasize the sound that each letter makes.

April Activities

Poem • After a Rainy Day •

After a very rainy day,
(Fingers fluttering downward)
When the sun begins to shine.
(Make large circle above head with arms)
I love to look up in the sky,
(One hand to forehead, head tilted back, looking upward)
To find a special sign.
(Hand still on forehead, move head as if looking around)

On lucky days, a giant arch,
(For the whole verse, slowly make a sweeping arch
with one arm)
With colors bright and bold,
Sweeps straight across a turquoise sky.
A treasure to behold.
("What is it?")

Group Activity
• Rainbow Experiments •

1. Try to obtain several prisms and hang them in a sunny window. Watch for rainbows to appear.
2. Different prisms will produce different sizes and numbers of rainbows. Ask children to point out the differences.
3. Try setting a pan of water in a sunny window. Rest a smooth-edged mirror in the pan, the bottom anchored with a piece of plasticine, so that the sunlight hits the mirror. Place a white sheet of paper opposite the mirror, between the pan and the window, so that a rainbow falls directly on the paper. Make the rainbow dance on the paper by gently moving the top of the mirror.

Creative Activity • Rainbow Glasses •

You'll need:

- egg cartons cut into double sections
- colored cellophane (available at arts and crafts stores)
- pipe cleaners
- white glue

1. Cut out the ends of egg-carton sections.
2. Children can glue colored cellophane pieces of their choice on the ends of the sections.
3. Attach pipe cleaners to the sides of the carton sections to make glasses.
4. Encourage children to share their glasses to see how the world looks in different colors.

Food Activity • Rainbow Dessert •

Create a delightful treat by layering fruit juice-flavored gelatin into a rainbow of color. If you begin the project in the morning of one day, it should be ready to eat by the next day.

You'll need:

- clear plastic or glass dessert containers
- box of unflavored gelatin
- a variety of fruit juices; e.g. grape, cranberry, apple, orange

1. Dissolve 1 packet of gelatin into 1 cup of warmed fruit juice.
2. Add an equal amount of cold juice to the mixture, stirring well.
3. Pour a thin layer of the mixture into the bottom of a clear container, and chill until gelled.
4. Repeat procedure for as many colored layers as desired; three layers generally prove successful. Be sure liquid is cool before it is poured on top of chilled layer.
5. Once final layer is chilled, enjoy as a refreshing snack after your rainbow dancing.

Recipe • Haroses •

(Jewish Passover)

This recipe recalls the bricks and mortar that the Hebrew people had to make as slaves under the pharaoh in ancient Egypt.

You'll need:

- 4 large apples, grated
- 1/4 cup grape juice
- 1 Tbsp. honey
- 1/4 cup walnuts, well-chopped
- 1/2 tsp. cinnamon
- matzohs or crackers

1. Mix first five ingredients together.
2. Spread on matzohs and enjoy.

Movement Activity
• Dancing with Rainbows •

1. Once prisms are hanging in a window (see Rainbow Experiments), gently swing them, and observe the rainbows dancing around your room. Play some music and dance with the rainbows.

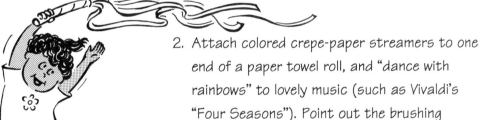

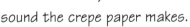

2. Attach colored crepe-paper streamers to one end of a paper towel roll, and "dance with rainbows" to lovely music (such as Vivaldi's "Four Seasons"). Point out the brushing sound the crepe paper makes.

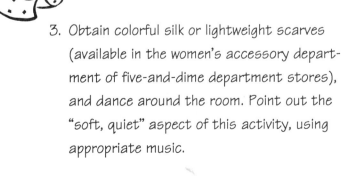

3. Obtain colorful silk or lightweight scarves (available in the women's accessory department of five-and-dime department stores), and dance around the room. Point out the "soft, quiet" aspect of this activity, using appropriate music.

Group Mural
• Flower Garden •

You'll need:

- a large roll of white mural paper
- brightly colored paint
- brushes
- plastic containers
- green pipe cleaners
- green construction paper

1. Lay out a length of mural paper and draw a line about halfway up the paper.
2. Have children choose a paint color and paint the palm of one hand.
3. With fingers either held together or spread out, have children place a hand-print on the line to make "flowers."
4. Stems and leaves can be painted in or glued on using green pipe cleaners or construction paper cutouts. Add birds, butterflies, insects, sun, and clouds to your mural.

Creative Activity • Go Fly a Kite •

This is another method of recycling paper bags.

You'll need:

- large paper grocery bags
- strong string or yarn cut into 3-foot lengths
- hole punch
- paint
- found materials
- crepe-paper streamers

1. Decorate your paper bags with paint and found materials.
2. Punch a hole in each of the four sides of the bag (not too close to the top edge). Tie string securely into holes.
3. Glue streamers to the bottom of your kite.
4. Take your kites on your next picnic.

May Special Event

May Day

In many countries May 1 is an important holiday. Some countries—Great Britain, for example—celebrate May Day to welcome the coming of summer. Other countries celebrate the contributions of all working people during May Day.

Activities

To Welcome Summer:

- Let the children be May Kings and May Queens. Cut out headbands in the shape of crowns and have the children decorate their crowns with crepe- or tissue-paper flowers they have made, with cut-out flowers, or with flower stickers. Attach streamers to a pole in your playground. Then let the May Kings and Queens dance around the Maypole, winding the streamers around the pole as they go.

- Tie bells and streamers to the children's wrists and ankles, put on some lively music, and encourage the children to participate in a May dance.

- Have a "May Tea Party" in the dramatic play center. Decorate with flowers and have children wear "dress-up" clothes. See suggestions for a Traditional Garden Party.

- Playing with hoops was a major part of May Day in the past. Take the hoops out onto the playground and encourage the children to create their own May Day dances with the hoops.

To Celebrate Work:

- Everyone has work to do, both in and out of the home. Discuss the work that children can do. Have available books that tell about various jobs and professions.

- Discuss the different kinds of work that parents do. Point out that men and women can and do perform the same jobs. All work is important. Discuss with the children what their lives would be like if there were no garbage collectors, doctors, or plumbers, for example.

- Invite two or three parents to class to talk about their occupations. Young children still have trouble accepting the fact that people can be Mother or Father and still be a doctor or a police officer. Discuss this with the children.

- From the dress-up corner, choose different clothes that suggest different kinds of jobs. Let the children dress up and have a Worker's Parade.

May Activities

Song • Springtime is Here and We're so Glad •

(Tune of "This is the Way")

Encourage the children to think of activities that they can add to this song.

Refrain
Springtime is here, and we're so glad,
We're so glad, we're so glad.
Springtime is here, and we're so glad,
'Cause we can play outside.

This is the way we skip our ropes,
Skip our ropes, skip our ropes.
This is the way we skip our ropes.
We love to play outside.

This is the way we ride our bikes,
Ride our bikes, ride our bikes.
This is the way we ride our bikes.
We love to play outside.

This is the way we dig in the sand,
Dig in the sand, dig in the sand.
This is the way we dig in the sand.
We love to play outside.

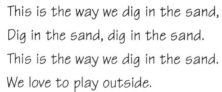

Group Activity • Traditional Garden Party •

This is a multifaceted activity that will culminate in a joyful outdoor event. Spend the week doing the following activities:

1. Make GARDEN PARTY HATS, TABLECLOTHS and DECORATIONS (instructions follow).
2. Collect adult dress-up clothes such as skirts, blouses, dresses, white gloves, belts, men's shirts, and ties.
3. Invite some special guests. Be sure to set a rain date.
4. Prepare FANCY SANDWICHES (instructions follow) and serve a fruit juice punch from a large bowl.
5. Arrange to have classical music playing for your party.
6. Decorate the yard with crepe-paper streamers.

GARDEN PARTY HATS

You'll need:

- colored bristol board
- small or medium paper doilies
- multicolored 5" square tissue-paper squares
- 1" squares of crepe paper or tissue paper

1. Cut bristol board into doughnut shapes to fit the crowns of children's heads.
2. Fit a large crepe-paper square over each child's head and slip doughnut shape over it. Remove the paper, turn it over carefully, and tape the edges to the underside of the bristol board brim.
3. Bunch small tissue-paper squares, and decorate the brim with doilies and the bunched "flowers."
4. You can make top hats with narrower brims and a crepe-paper band.

TABLECLOTHS

You'll need:

- colored newsprint or commercial paper tablecloth
- a variety of cookie cutters
- tempera paint
- shallow containers to hold paint for dipping
- crayons

1. Dip cookie cutters into tempera paint and decorate the paper with prints.
2. When paint is dry, trace children's handprints at random on the paper.
3. Tape newsprint together to create tablecloth size desired.

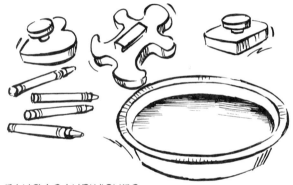

ROOM/YARD DECORATIONS

The best decorations are crepe-paper streamers wrapped around, taped to, tied to, or woven through any suitable place. When attached by one end, they look lovely moving in a breeze.

FANCY SANDWICHES

You'll need:

- loaves of thinly-sliced bread, crust trimmed, if desired (white, whole wheat, oat, multigrain, etc.)
- a variety of sandwich fillings (tuna salad, egg salad, cream cheese, peanut butter, jam, etc.)
- margarine or butter, room temperature

For ribbon sandwiches:

1. Butter bread slices.
2. Spread fillings on bread slices and stack 3 or 4 high, alternating fillings.
3. Cover well with waxed paper and damp tea towels, and refrigerate.
4. Slice just before serving.

For spiral sandwiches:

1. Butter and spread filling on a slice of trimmed bread.
2. Roll tightly, cover as above, and refrigerate.
3. Slice before serving.

Creative Activity • Gift for Mom
• Portrait Pendants

You'll need:

- a batch of baker's clay
- 2 cups flour
- 1 cup salt
- 1 cup water
- a few drops food coloring

- small photo of each child that can be cut out
- drinking glass or round cookie cutter
- uncoated paper clips
- cookie sheet
- markers/glue/glitter
- curling ribbon
- wrapping or tissue paper

Mix all ingredients and knead for several minutes.

1. Roll out dough to approximately 1/4" thick.
2. Cut circle out of dough using glass circle or cookie cutter.
3. Cut circle around child's face in photo, slightly smaller than dough circle.
4. Place photo in center of dough, and fold edges around edges of photo.
5. Place paper clip in top edge, making sure it is well embedded in dough.
6. Bake at 300° F for approximately 1 hour.
7. Leave frame plain, decorate with markers, or paint on white glue and sprinkle with glitter.
8. Tie ribbon onto paper clip and wrap for Mother's Day.

Outing • Spring Flower I.D. •

You'll need:

- pictures from seed catalogs or garden center fliers
- cardboard or construction paper

Take pleasure in the arrival of spring with a walk in your neighborhood. Before going out, mount pictures of flowers on cardboard and use them to help you identify the spring flowers you see along the way. For activity time, make name cards and duplicates of your flower pictures to do a tabletop matching activity.

June Special Event

Environment Day

There are many activities that can be done with young children to foster a caring attitude toward the environment. One of the most important goals is to help the children develop an appreciation of nature. From this foundation, it is easy to move to positive action.

Activities

- Provide environmental games for your classroom. "A Beautiful Place" by Family Pastimes in Perth, Ontario, Canada, is one game that is suitable for 4- to 7-year-olds.

- Take a nature walk with the children. Make note of all the interesting things you see—from plants and animals to insects and birds. Make note also of garbage, graffiti, and so on that you observe. At circle time discuss with the children what you saw on the walk. Did you see anything that indicated a lack of care for the Earth?

- Have a special container where children can place partly used paper and other materials. Recycle the materials by using them in craft projects.

- Place a metal garbage can in the playground for refuse. Let the children paint designs on it with tempera paint. (You will probably want to store such an attractive container inside to protect it from the rain, and take it out with the other small items of playground equipment.)

- Plan a garbage-free picnic. Have children bring food in reusable plastic containers, and use flasks or reusable plastic bottles for beverages. Provide cloth napkins for the children instead of paper ones.

- Use recycled paper to make Happy Earth Day cards for family members and friends.

- Have a Happy Earth Day party. Decorate the classroom with flowers and decorations made from your leftover paper container. Make a Happy Earth Day banner to hang in the classroom. Use washable plastic dishes for your snacks, and let the children help to wash them.

See "Environment" section for more ideas about helping to care for the environment.

June Activities

Song
• Hippity Hoppity Froggie •

(Tune of "The Eensy Weensy Spider")

The hippity hoppity froggie went swimming in the pond.
(Swimming action with arms)

Looking for some insects, of which he was quite fond.
(Make binoculars with hands, hold up to eyes, look around)

Out flipped his tongue
(Left palm under right elbow, flip arm down, hand open)

To catch a tiny fly.
(Close hand, flip arm up)

Then the hippity hoppity froggie croaked, and hopped on by.
(Hop like a frog)

Group Activity • Plant a Tree •

After choosing the best spot in your yard for a new tree, take a trip to the garden center to purchase a tree seedling or bush. Get help from the staff to choose the variety best suited to your classroom conditions.

Certain small bushes can be planted in a large planter if necessary. Children can tend their tree or bush all season and observe its growth and changes over the course of the year.

Finger Play • My Garden •

(a traditional verse)

This is my garden, I'll rake it with care.
(Raking motion)
And then some flower seeds I'll place in there.
(Pretend to plant seeds)
The sun will shine,
(Make a circle above head with arms)
The rain will fall.
(Flutter fingers in a downward motion)
And my garden will blossom and grow straight
and tall.
(Place heels of hands together, fingers rounded
and pointed up, in a flower shape)

Creative Activity • Binoculars •

Take these binoculars on your next nature walk. Although they are "just pretend," they do encourage
the children to take a closer look at nature's bounty. While outdoors, provide some challenges, such
as using the binoculars to examine tree bark, blades of grass, small wildflowers, the surface of a rock,
or a fallen feather.

You'll need:

- two toilet-paper rolls for each child
- hole punch
- glue/masking tape
- markers, crayons, small bits of scrap paper or
  fabric
- yarn

1. Join the rolls by wrapping them together with
   masking tape.
2. Punch one hole 1" from end of both rolls.
3. Decorate rolls with available materials.
4. Make a neckstrap by tying yarn to holes at end of
   binoculars.

Creative Activity • Kid Cars

These vehicles add a different dimension to outdoor play. If the children are having difficulty playing constructively, help with some ideas such as setting up a car wash (don't use real water), going out to buy a new car, going to and from work (don't forget to park your cars before going in to work).

You'll need:

- child-size cardboard cartons
- paint
- string
- small paper or tin plates
- paper fasteners/masking tape
- decorative materials such as yarn, buttons, crepe paper

1. Cut the flaps off the bottom of the carton, and cut a child-size circle out of the top. Poke four holes in the top to add string later.
2. Have children paint and decorate their cars in their own way.
3. Add paper plates as headlights, and put the string into the holes for shoulder straps.
4. Some additional features can be added, such as paper license plates, a flip-up trunk in the back, or a paper plate steering wheel on the top.

Recipe • Watermelon-Strawberry Pops •

By the middle of June, local strawberries will begin to appear. Take your group to a pick-your-own berry farm or farmer's market, then turn your harvest into a quick cooler for tomorrow's snack.

You'll need:

- 1 quart strawberries
- 2 cups seeded watermelon pieces
- 2 cups apple juice
- small paper cups and wooden sticks
- blender
- cookie sheet

1. Slice berries and reserve 1/2 of the quart.
2. Blend watermelon, juice, and 1/2 of the sliced berries
3. Pour mixture into cups labeled with children's names, drop in several slices of strawberry, and place cups on cookie sheet.
4. Put in freezer. Insert wooden sticks into cups when mixture is partially frozen.
5. When frozen, pass cups under warm water to loosen pops.

Outdoor (or Indoor) Activity • Ring Toss

You'll need:

- wooden clothespins
- a sturdy gift box, 3–4" deep
- rubber mason jar rings
- markers or paint

1. Color clothespins with markers or paint.
2. Make holes in the box into which clothespins will fit securely. Allow clothespins to poke up 2". (Number and spacing of holes will depend on abilities of children.)
3. Place clothespins in holes.
4. Children toss rings over pins, trying to ring as many on as possible.
5. Children can try to get 1 ring on each pin, or choose 1 or 2 colors to try to get all of their rings over.

Father's Day Activity • Pretzel for Pop •

You'll need:

- frozen whole-wheat bread dough
- coarse salt
- 1 egg white
- 1 tsp. water
- cookie sheet
- small doilies
- small paper plates
- crayons/markers to decorate edges of plates
- plastic wrap
- ribbon

1. Cut thawed dough into 8–10 pieces.
2. Each child rolls a piece of dough into a coil.
3. With the help of the teacher, each child forms the dough into the initial letter of his or her dad's name.
4. Place letters on the cookie sheet, cover with a moist towel, and allow dough to rise for approximately 20 minutes.
5. Beat egg white and water together, brush onto pretzels, and sprinkle lightly with salt.
6. Bake at 350° F for approximately 20 minutes.
7. Decorate edges of paper plates.
8. Place doilies in center, place pretzels on doilies, cover with plastic wrap, and tie on ribbons.

Independence Day, U.S.A.

July 4 is the celebration of a historical event, but for very young children the emphasis should be on the celebration. This is a good time to plan a Happy Birthday U.S.A. party!

Activities

- Discuss how Native Americans were already here when other groups of people crossed the ocean to come to this country. Display a map of the world, and mark with flags or colored dots the areas that the children or their ancestors came from. Talk about how some people have been here for a long time, and some have just recently arrived.

- Ask parents to loan you special music, articles, costumes, and so on, from their countries of origin or ancestry. Encourage the parents to visit the classroom, and teach a song or a game from their country. Serve a traditional snack suggested by the parents.

- For a snack, have vanilla-flavored yogurt, fresh strawberries or raspberries, and blueberries. The children can decorate their dishes of white yogurt with the red and blue berries.

- Make hats of red, white, and blue construction paper. Have the children decorate their hats with red, white, and blue crayons or small bits of construction paper. Make red, white, and blue crepe-paper vests. Have the children put on their hats and vests, get out the rhythm instruments, and have a parade.

- Color a United States flag on ten pieces of cardboard or construction paper in gradually increasing sizes. The children can then arrange the flags according to size.

- Make star hand puppets. Using a template of a star large enough to fit a child's hand, cut two stars for each child out of white felt. Have the children glue the edges of their stars together, leaving open enough space to insert their hands. Have the children use their star puppets while they sing the national anthem.

July Activities

Outdoor Activity • Bubble Days •

Herald in summer with some fun experiments with bubbles.

You'll need:

- good-quality dish detergent (such as Joy)
- serving trays
- drinking straws cut in 3" pieces
- household string cut in 3" lengths
- wire hangers
- frozen juice cans
- masking tape
- glycerine (from pharmacy)

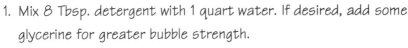

1. Mix 8 Tbsp. detergent with 1 quart water. If desired, add some glycerine for greater bubble strength.

2. Cover several outdoor tables with newspaper, and place trays of soap mixture on each table. Each tray can have a different type of bubble blower. Try these bubble toys:

   - conventional ones from commercial bubbles
   - different shapes made from lightweight clothes hangers or other wire
   - straws
   - juice cans opened at both ends (tape edges for safety)

3. Careful dipping, gentle blowing, and slow movement of bubble toys through the air will ensure success.

4. Bathing suits and a hose will ease the cleanup process.

Poem • Deep-Sea Diver •

If I were a deep-sea diver, what things would I see below,
Under the blue-green waters, where fishes swim so low?

Would I see a giant sunken ship, with treasure out of sight?
Or schools of multicolored fish, their scales just shining bright?

I'd love to hug an octopus, or hold a dolphin's hand.
If a sharp-toothed shark swam close to me, I'd hide in a pit of sand.

When I grow up I think I'll learn, to swim beneath the sea,
So I can meet sea creatures, and they'll make friends with me.

Table Activity • Gone Fishing •

| You'll need: |

- cardboard box with top and bottom cut out
- cardboard cut into different sizes of fish
  shapes (draw eyes and fins with crayon)
- paper clips
- fishing pole made by tying a magnet to the end
  of a small stick with string
- small containers or shoebox lids for sorting fish

1. Place paper clips on fish shapes.
2. Decorate outside of box with an underwater
   scene.
3. Place box on a table and place fish inside.
4. Using their poles, have children go fishing
   with magnets.
5. Sort fish in containers by size.

VARIATION:
Put letters of the alphabet or numerals on fish.

Creative Activity • Floating Fish •

You'll need:

- large fingerpaint paper
- cardboard cut into a variety of fish shapes no more than 1/2 the size of the fingerpaint paper
- stapler
- small strips of newspaper
- green and blue construction paper
- green tissue paper
- craft paper
- heavy thread/sewing needles

1. Have children paint their own colorful designs on fingerpaint paper (at easel or table). Allow to dry well.

2. Fold paintings in half (unpainted side inside), choose a fish pattern, trace around it, and cut out fish shape. (Older children can do all of these steps themselves.)

3. Staple or glue edges halfway around bodies of fish shapes, stuff with newspaper strips, and finish stapling or gluing around edges. Ensure that children's names are on their fishes.

4. For the background, paint streaks of blue and green on craft paper

5. Sew thread into backs of fish, and mount at random on background.

6. Cut green construction paper into various plant shapes, and glue among the fish.

7. To add depth, bunch large squares of tissue paper and glue them to the background.

8. Mount the mural on a wall. Children may want to name their fish.

VARIATION:

Hang several fish on different lengths of string from a clothes hanger, and hang fish as mobiles around the room.

Indoor or Outdoor Activity
• A Lemonade Stand •

- Work together to set up a lemonade stand for the group.
- Divide jobs for setting up and running your stand.
- Work toward the special day by making signs and play money, arranging a staffing schedule and some extra adult help for supervision. Invite parents and other visitors.

Recipe • Cool as a Cucumber Dip •

Plan this recipe as a cooler for a hot summer day.

You'll need:

- 2 or more cucumbers, peeled
- 1 16-ounce container of plain lowfat yogurt or sour cream
- 1 tsp. each of dried parsley and/or dill
- individual paper cups for dipping
- blender

1. Blend one cucumber with other ingredients until smooth.
2. Peel and slice other cucumber into spears and disks and arrange on plate. Serve with cups of dip.
3. Serve as a snack or appetizer before lunch.
4. While eating, discuss the meaning of the expression "cool as a cucumber."

Outdoor Activity
• The Pitter Patter of Little Feet Mural •

You'll need:

- craft paper roll
- 2 chairs
- 2 or 3 paint colors/paint brushes
- bucket of warm soapy water
- sponge or cloth

1. Spread a long piece of craft paper onto a hard surface.
2. Place a chair (and adult) at either end of the paper.
3. One child chooses a color and sits down at one end of the paper. The child's feet are then painted with the color of his or her choice. Another child or adult can help with painting.
4. The child walks to the end of the paper and sits down, then the teacher helps to wash the child's feet. Some children prefer to have an adult accompany them from one end to the other.
5. When all the children have had a turn, let the mural dry, and mount it inside the school.

August Special Event

Circus Days, North America

August is a perfect time to have a circus. It can be done indoors or out, depending on the weather. Allow a week or two to plan and make the necessary props. Use library books with colorful pictures of circuses to give you ideas. Display the books for the children to enjoy and to generate a discussion about the circus.

Activities

- Young children enjoy dressing up as clowns, but they need to be led into it slowly. As a beginning activity, make a tracing of each child's body on a piece of craft paper. Help the children cut out their body shapes. Then let them color their figures as clowns, using bright stripes and polka dots for the clothes. Last, let the children draw clown faces on their figures.

- Put a funny nose on the clown. For the clown's face, cut a large circle or oval out of white Bristol board. Draw in clown eyes, mouth, cheeks, eyebrows, and so on. Add a construction paper hat. Attach the clown face to the wall at child height. Cut out a round red nose from construction paper for each child. Put the child's name on the nose. Make a ring of masking tape, sticky side out, for the back. Children, in turn, are blindfolded or close their eyes and try to stick their clown noses closest to the "right" spot on the clown's face.

- At this point, the children may be ready to dress up as clowns. Have available several mirrors (made with safety glass). A long mirror placed on a table at child height works best. Have an adult model the activity by painting a clown's face on his or her own face with water-based face paints. Then, give each child the paints to create their own clown's face if they wish. Use old clothes such as brightly colored pajamas for clown costumes.

- Get out the rhythm instruments and play some lively music. Let the children have a circus parade around the classroom.

- Set out balance beams or flat boards for the children to use for "tightrope walking." You can also make "tightropes" on the floor with masking tape for the children to walk along.

- Make popcorn for a snack.

August Activities

Song
• Mr. Grasshopper •

Hey, Mr. Grasshopper,
How high can you jump?
As high as that fence,
Or perhaps a tall stump?

Hey, Mr. Grasshopper,
I love your disguise.
You hide in long grass,
Then jump out and . . . SURPRISE !

Outdoor Activity • Texture Rubbing Collages •

Pack a lunch, put on good walking shoes, and tune up those eagle eyes. This excursion requires a leisurely pace.

You'll need:

- a variety of wax crayons with paper peeled off
- lots of 8 1/2 x 11" white paper, medium weight
- scissors
- glue
- construction paper

1. While walking to your lunch spot, encourage children to watch out for, and gently feel, all different kinds of surfaces. Have them describe the textures they feel. Some suggestions: tree bark, brick/stone walls, pavement, park bench seat, metal plaque on a building.
2. Have children choose a surface to rub, place the paper on top of the surface, and rub over it using the SIDE of a crayon.
3. When you return to school, set up a table with glue, scissors, construction paper, and your rubbings.
4. Have children cut the rubbings into different shapes and sizes and collage them onto the construction paper background.
5. When collages are complete, look at them during circle time as a group, and try to remember which objects produced the different textures.

Recipe • Yogurt Pops •

You'll need:

- one 16-ounce container of lowfat plain yogurt
- fresh fruit pieces of your choice
- small paper cups
- wooden sticks
- blender
- cookie sheet
- small pitcher

1. Blend yogurt and fruit together.
2. Using small pitcher or measuring cup, each child pours mixture into a cup marked with his or her name.
3. Place filled cups on cookie sheet, and put into freezer.
4. When mixture is partially frozen, have children place sticks into their own cups (sticks should stand up easily in center).
5. When frozen, release pops by quickly dipping cups into pan of warm water.
6. Wash and save cups and sticks for future use.

Group Activity • Let's Have a Parade •

For some fun on a sunshiny day, put on clothes from the dramatic play corner, sing "The Ants Go Marching" and "Knees Up Mother Brown", and play the noisemakers described below.

You'll need:

- toilet-paper or paper-towel rolls, or thin paper plates
- dried beans
- paint, crayons, markers
- scrap paper/glue
- crepe-paper streamers
- stapler

1. Children can decorate the paper rolls or outside of paper plates with the materials provided. Let dry.
2. Staple closed one end of the roll, add beans, and staple the other end.
3. If you are using paper plates, place beans on inside of plate, fold in half, and staple around curved edge.
4. Streamers can be stapled or glued onto one corner.
5. March around the yard, then sit under a tree and cool off with a yogurt pop.

Circle Game
• Let's Hang Out the Wash •

1. Glue all the letters of the alphabet to the top portion of wooden clothespins.
2. Hang pins on a "clothesline" mounted in the room or outdoors.
3. Gather articles of clothing for each letter, or paste magazine pictures onto construction paper.
4. Children can take turns choosing items from a laundry basket and placing them with the correct initial letter.
5. If some items of clothing are impossible to represent, fill in with any other object.

Outdoor Activity • Shadow Shapes •

Do this activity in the yard on a warm, sunny day. Older children can work in pairs, younger children can work individually with the teacher while the others play in the yard. Provide pails of water for washing up afterward.

You'll need:
- brown craft paper rolls
- crayons/markers
- paint/found materials

1. Cut pieces of craft paper to accommodate the height of the children. Place the craft paper in a sunny location in the yard.
2. Have children stand at the bottom of the paper so their shadows fall on paper, positioning arms and legs as desired.
3. Each partner takes turns tracing around the shadow of the other with a crayon or marker.
4. The children can then paint in clothes and facial features. When the paint is dry, they can paste on belts, buttons, pockets, and so on, using found materials.

Creative Activity • Corncob Prints •

You'll need:

- several cobs of corn
- corn holders
- several trays of tempera paint
- white paper

1. Break corn into a variety of sizes; push corn holders into ends.
2. Dip cobs into paint.
3. Roll cobs in different directions over paper. Children can allow paint to dry and print new colors over previously painted areas.
4. When finished, thoroughly wash corn and place in compost, or leave out for animals to eat.

Outdoor Activity
• Mini-Golf/Croquet Course •

You'll need:

- corrugated board from cardboard boxes
- wire hangers
- heavy-duty silver duct tape (available at hardware stores)
- paint

1. Cut 5–10 arch shapes out of corrugated board.
2. Have children paint one side of each arch however they wish.
3. Open hangers, bend into arches, and tape onto backs of cardboard arches, leaving approximately 3" at each end to stick into the ground.
4. Make your course by placing arches throughout yard.
5. For mallets, ask families to contribute mallets from home or use toy golf clubs or racquets.
6. Provide a variety of balls, such as golf, foam, soccer, and hollow plastic, and have children experiment by using different types of mallets with different balls.

VARIATIONS:

1. Paint numbers in sequence and have the children follow the course in order.
2. Add a variety of items to your course such as large juice cans with the ends removed, hula hoops, and cardboard boxes with arched openings at either end.

September Special Event

Rosh Hashanah, a Jewish holiday

Rosh Hashanah, the Jewish New Year, is celebrated on two days in September or early October (the date changes because it is based on the lunar calendar). A shofar (ram's horn) is blown to call the people to prayer. A special meal is eaten at sundown. The meal includes ladder-shaped challah (bread), which signifies prayers ascending to God, or round challah, which signifies the end of the old year and the beginning of the new. Sometimes the challah has raisins in it to symbolize a sweet year to come. Slices of apple are dipped in honey to ensure a year of sweetness.

Activities

- Make Rosh Hashanah cards. Use blue, yellow, and white construction paper. Use pictures of apples, Stars of David, or brown construction paper cut-outs of challah.

- Teach the children the phrases Shanah Tovah, meaning "a good year," or L' Shanah Tovah, meaning "Have a Happy New Year."

- Invite families who celebrate this holiday to visit the classroom to discuss this special time of year.

- Slice the top off an apple, and scoop the core and seeds out to make a honey bowl. Dip slices of apple, or chunks of challah, into the honey, to ensure a sweet year.

- At circle time, talk about sweet and sour tastes. Have samples of each for the children to taste.

- Ask a parent to come to the classroom to make challah with the children. Make one or two large loaves, or give each of the children a bit of dough and let them make their own small shapes.

- Discuss the fact that sundown marks the beginning of all Jewish holidays. Have the children draw night and day pictures.

September Activities

Poem • Five Apples •

Five apples round and rosy,
Hanging in a tree,
They sat together cozy,
Sipping morning tea.

Some children skipped by singing.
The apples called with glee,
"Won't you come and join us,
And taste our recipe?"

The children climbed up nimbly,
Each sat beside a friend.
They talked and munched on biscuits,
Told stories 'til day's end.

The moon appeared quite quickly,
To everyone's surprise.
They hugged and kissed their buddies,
Then waved their last goodbyes.

Circle Activity
• The Name Game •

This activity helps children to meet one another at the beginning of a new school session, or to greet old friends after a summer break.

1. One child thinks of a three- or four-word sentence using his or her name, and an action starting with the same initial sound, adding "and" at the end. For example, "Billy bites bagels and . . ."

2. The next child thinks of a sentence and adds it to the previous child's sentence. For example, "Billy bites bagels and Jason jumps on jellybeans and . . ."

3. Continue to the end of the group ensuring that as the sentence gets longer, the children help each other to remember previous additions where necessary.

Creative Activity • Fingerprint Pictures •

This month is spent becoming familiar with new friends and gaining confidence. Create opportunities for children to talk about themselves and their families. Start a bulletin board of family photos, and photos of the children doing different activities; encourage children talk about their photos. Emphasize that everyone is unique and special, even down to our fingertips.

Every child can discover his or her own unique fingerprints with the following activity:

You'll need:

- small containers of tempera paint (thick)
- fingerpaint paper, 8 1/2" x 11"
- bowls of soapy water/towel

1. Children create pictures using fingertips only. Encourage them to dip fingertips CAREFULLY into the paint, and dab carefully onto the paper, so that they will be able to see the designs of their prints.

2. Point out the shape of each print, and the designs produced by the lines of the children's fingertips.

3. Turn your prints into creatures by adding legs, feelers, tails, etc.

Creative Activity
• Monarch Butterflies •

Observe the mass migration of the monarch butterflies from Canada and the Northern United States to Southern California and Mexico for the winter.

You'll need:

- paper
- black and orange paint (thick)
- paintbrush
- cardboard pattern for butterfly cut in half
  (make sure it fits within the dimensions of your paper)

1. Have children fold their paper in half and open.
2. Dab blobs of paint on one-half of paper near the fold. Use more orange than black.
3. Fold paper in half again. Rub hand over paper to spread paint.
4. Open, and add more paint if necessary.
5. When paint is completely dry, fold again and trace butterfly pattern.
6. Cut out butterfly shapes, and create a mass migration by mounting the children's monarchs together on the wall or a bulletin board.

Food Activity • Apple Activities •

In September a huge variety of apples appears on the scene. Take your group to an open air market or the produce section of the grocery store, and purchase a mixture of sizes, shapes, and colors of these nutritious and juicy morsels.

1. The children can take responsibility for washing the apples.
2. Spend some time comparing the size, shape, and color of all the varieties you have purchased.
3. Cut some apples horizontally, and some vertically in half; compare the different appearances (point out the star in the middle of horizontal cuts), including the differences in color of the pulp.
4. Make apple-print pictures by pressing your apple halves onto a sponge soaking in tempera paint in a container. Note the different designs they make. When finished, wash apples well, and place outdoors for animals preparing for winter.
5. Make open- or closed-face sandwiches by coring and cutting apples in 1/2"-thick rounds. Use peanut butter and cream cheese as spread choices.

Snack • Dried Apples •

You'll need:

- enough apples for your group
- kitchen string
- knife/apple corer
- honey/maple syrup

1. Peel and core apples. Save scraps for compost or snacks.
2. Slice apples into 1/4" rings.
3. String apples through hole, leaving space between them.
4. Hang strings in a warm, out-of-the-way location.
5. Dry for one week.
6. When rings are ready to eat, provide individual bowls of honey or maple syrup for dipping. Or take them along for a snack on your next group outing.

Group Activity • Appreciate Books Week •

(International Literacy Day)

Join with UNESCO'S (United Nations Educational, Scientific, and Cultural Organization) recognition of the world's illiteracy problems; over 25% of adults are unable to read or write.

Do the following activities over the course of the week:

1. Discuss what illiteracy is, and why books are so important.
2. Make up a GROUP STORY on any topic children choose. Be sure to explain "sequence of events" as the order in which things happen (first, second, third, etc.). Have children take turns creating parts of the story. Using one piece of chart paper, write down the children's words for each part of the story, and invite children to illustrate each part. When the story is complete, choose a title. Mount your story in sequence, and read it as a group at circletime.
3. Children can write their own books during activity time. Put out special "book-writing paper." Each child can choose a favorite topic and do the illustrations, while you write their words for them. Make sure the book's title, author, and illustrator are on the cover. After the books are bound (with staples), the children can read their stories to each other.
4. Make up a variety of picture cards from magazine pictures that the children can use to invent their own stories at circletime and/or activity time. Have paper available to write down the children's words when necessary.

Craft • Wildflower Placemats •

Remember the beauty of summer by collecting and preserving growing things. Now is an appropriate time to pick flowers, since they will soon be dying back for winter.

Plan a group outing to a meadow or field to collect a variety of wildflowers, weeds, and grasses.

You'll need:

- waxed paper
- newspaper
- wildflowers and weeds
- iron

1. Place a piece of waxed paper, waxy side up, on several thicknesses of newspaper.
2. Make an arrangement of growing things, leaving space around edges and between items.
3. Cover arrangement with waxy side of second piece of waxed paper.
4. Cover arrangement with newspaper, and iron at medium-high until both sides are well joined. (Children can help with ironing if closely supervised.)
5. Use placemats for a snack or lunch, then hide away to bring out on a chilly winter day.

October Special Event

Diwali, Hindu Festival of Lights

Diwali is a 5-day Hindu celebration in honor of Lakshmi, the goddess of Light. It is also a nonsecular celebration in which people of Indian origin observe the beginning of winter. It is a holiday of worship, special food, and entertainment. Diyas, small clay lamps, are lit and placed in the windows to guide Lakshmi to people's homes to provide prosperity and good luck.

Activities

- Make small lamps out of play dough or clay. Use pipe cleaner for the wicks and yellow construction paper as flames. Display the lamps on the window sills in the classroom.

- Make garlands of tissue-paper flowers to hang in the doorways in honor of Lakshmi.

- Invite a parent to come to the classroom to make simple Diwali sweets with the children, or purchase the sweets at a local bakery. Serve the treats to the children at snack time. Chapati, or Indian bread, also makes a nice snack.

- Hindus make colorful good luck designs of rice flour to set near the entrances to a building or room. Have the children make their own designs with glue, construction paper, and designs on the floor near the entrance of the classroom.

- Tell the children that many Indian foods are very spicy. Bring in curry, cumin, coriander, cardamom, and turmeric. Pass the spices around at circle time. Have the children carefully smell the spices. Then use the spices to make a collage by spreading glue on construction paper and sprinkling the various spices on the glue. Encourage the children to experience the smells of the spice collage.

- The timing of this holiday is tied to the phases of the moon. Use yellow construction paper to make half-moon and whole-moon pins or pendants. Draw faces on the moons. Then add string, or tape a safety pin to the back of each moon face. Wear the moon-face pins for your Diwali festival.

- Cut out 10 pairs of oil lamps from construction paper, each pair in a different color. Then let the children match the lamps according to color. For another activity, draw an equivalent number (1 to 10) of black dots on each pair of lamps, and have the children match the 2 lamps that have the same number of dots.

October Activities

Song • All the Leaves are Fluttering •

(Tune of "Mary Had a Little Lamb")

All the leaves are fluttering, fluttering, fluttering.
All the leaves are fluttering,
In the gusty wind.
(Flutter fingers all around)

Now the leaves are falling down, falling down, falling down.
Now the leaves are falling down,
To the chilly ground.
(Flutter fingers in a downward motion)

Hear the leaves go crunch, crunch, crunch,
Crunch, crunch, crunch, crunch, crunch, crunch,
Hear the leaves go crunch, crunch, crunch,
Underneath your feet.
(Pretend to crunch leaves with feet)

See our neighbors rake, rake, rake,
Rake, rake, rake, rake, rake, rake.
(Use raking motion)
See our neighbors rake, rake, rake,
Into leafy piles.
(Children pretend to jump into piles,
and throw leaves into the air)

Poem • Leafy Dancers •

Who are those dancers way up there?

Gently waltzing through the air.

Their golden costumes swirling 'round,

With arms outstretched, they're drifting down.

Group Activity • Food Collection •

(World Food Day)

This is an opportunity to draw children's attention to world food shortages. A map or globe can be used to show which countries around the world are experiencing shortages. Emphasize that families in their own communities experience food shortages, as well.

THINGS TO DO:

1. Take a trip to the neighborhood food store to choose some items suitable for donation to your local food bank.

2. If you feel it is appropriate for your group, send a note home explaining World Food Day. Request a donation of a packaged or canned food item for the group's collection.

3. Try to arrange for a food bank representative to pick up your group's items and talk to the children. Better yet, visit the food bank to deliver the items yourselves.

Recipe • Squash Rings •

You'll need:

- 2 or 3 acorn squashes, sliced horizontally into rings
- 2 Tbsp. honey and 2 Tbsp. butter or margarine, melted together over medium heat
- pastry brush
- tin plates
- cookie sheet(s)

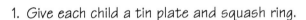

1. Give each child a tin plate and squash ring.
2. Have children take turns brushing the honey mixture onto both sides of the squash ring.
3. Place plates on cookie sheet(s), and bake at 350° F for 1/2 hour or until soft enough to eat.
4. Brush rings with mixture once or twice during cooking.
5. Serve as vegetable for lunch.

Halloween Recipe • Harvest Brew •

You'll need:

- enough apple cider for your group
- ground cinnamon to taste
- dash of ground cloves or float some cloves in mixture
- one cinnamon stick for each mug

1. Warm all ingredients except cinnamon sticks together on a low to medium heat. Keep stirring. Do not boil.
2. Place cinnamon sticks into mugs, and pour in mixture.
3. Enjoy at snacktime when cool enough to drink.

Creative Activity
• Hats, Hats, Hats •

As the weather gets cooler, and the children spend more time indoors, beef up your dramatic play corner with a choice of headgear. All of these activities can be set up at a craft table for children to do themselves:

TOP HAT: Cut a circle out of black paper, and cut a large hole in the center. With another piece of black paper, make 3-cm cuts along the bottom, 3 cm apart, and staple into a cylinder that will fit inside the hole in the black circle. Tape cuts in the cylinder to the inside of the brim.

CROWN: Cut zig-zags in bristol board strips (10–15 cm wide); cover with tinfoil; decorate with glue and found materials while still flat. When dry, staple ends together to fit each child.

ANIMAL EARS: using a narrow hair band or cardboard headband, glue the bottoms of felt or construction paper ears onto the band.

Craft • Leaf Rubbings •

You'll need:

- autumn leaves
- colored newsprint
- crayons

1. Place a leaf, vein side up, between two pieces of newsprint held together with paper clips.

2. Rub over top layer of paper with side of crayon to get impression of leaf.

3. Place leaves in other spots and rub again.

November Special Event

Native Thanksgiving (Harvest Moon)

Explain to the children that this traditional celebration was very important in the past when Native Americans hunted, gathered, and stored their food for the winter. Discuss the fact that because there are many different nations of Native Americans, many of the customs are also different, but that fall harvest celebrations are popular around the world. At this time of the year, many people give thanks to the earth, grass, plants, birds, and animals.

Activities

- Visit a museum to see displays of Native American artifacts. Be sure that the children understand that the exhibits are examples of how some Native American people lived long ago. Make sure that the children understand that the way that past lifestyles are portrayed is not necessarily the way that Native Americans live today. Contemporary Native Americans live on reservations, in cities, in small towns, and in rural areas. Many of today's Native Americans keep ancient traditions alive in modern celebrations.

- Use brightly colored beads to make necklaces. Tell children that some Native Americans use beads to make intricate patterns on their clothes, baskets, and tools. If available,

show pictures of Native American beadwork. Let the children string the beads in simple patterns that they create.

- Make paper-bag vests. Using large brown paper bags, start at the open end and cut up the middle of one of the large panels to the bottom of the bag. Then cut away a portion of the bottom to make the head and neck opening. Next cut sleeve holes in each side. Crumple the bag to make it look like worn leather, and decorate your vest with designs in earth colors.

- Long ago, people stored their food in pots and leather bags. Show the children pictures of pottery with carved or painted designs. Use air-drying clay to make pots, and popsicle sticks or other safe tools to create designs in the soft clay. If you prefer, paint the pottery with designs after the clay is dry.

- Do a drum dance of thanksgiving. Make drums out of plastic containers, or use your circle drums and maracas. Encourage different beats, such as loud/soft or fast/slow. For variation, have children use their drums to beat out the syllables in their names.

November Activities

Song • Canada Geese •

(Tune of "The Ants Go Marching In")

The Canada Geese are flying by, Hoorah, Hoorah.
The Canada Geese are in the sky, Hoorah, Hoorah.
Down south they go when the cold wind blows,
They sneak away before it snows.
They'll return again to the north, in the spring, when it's warm.
Honk, Honk, Honk.

The Canada Geese are flying by, Hoorah, Hoorah.
The Canada Geese are in the sky, Hoorah, Hoorah.
In tidy V-shaped rows they fly,
They're ringing out their honking cry,
They'll return again to the north, in the spring, when it's warm.
Honk, Honk, Honk.
Return again to the north, in the spring, when its warm.
Honk, Honk, Honk, Honk.

Outdoor Activity
• Nature Walk •

In early November, before the snow falls, dress up in warm clothes and go on a search in a wooded area for some natural items to keep on hand for decorations and crafts during the winter. Make sure each child has a bag for collecting, but explain that everything will be put together on your return, for sharing at another time. While you are walking, watch and listen for signs of animals preparing for winter. Try to pick up a good selection of pinecones for a December craft.

Poem • Winter's Here •

The leaves have fallen to the ground,
A bite is in the air.
The winter wind has blown its sound.
All creatures must prepare,

With winter coats and hidden food,
And well-built homes deep in the wood.
Some birds fly south, some stay right here.
Bears start a long sleep this time of year.

So find your mitts, dig up those boots.
It's time to wear your winter suits.
The snow may fall, prepare yourselves.
And put those woollies on your shelves.

Craft • Bird Feeders •

FEEDER 1

You'll need:

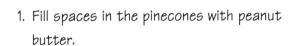

- pinecones
- sunflower seeds
- string
- peanut butter
- knife

1. Fill spaces in the pinecones with peanut butter.
2. Roll firmly in sunflower seeds.
3. Tie string to pinecone end, and hang outdoors.

FEEDER 2

You'll need:

- milk cartons
- string
- birdseed
- sticks or straws

1. Cut out side of milk carton.
2. Attach stick as a perch for birds.
3. Tie string to the top, fill with bird seed, and hang outdoors.

REMEMBER:

- Once birds discover your feeders, they will depend on them as a food source throughout the winter. Set up a group schedule for checking and refilling feeders on a regular basis.
- Place feeders where they are safe from squirrels and neighborhood pets. They should be within easy reach for children to refill them.
- This is an opportunity to observe nature. Keep a book on hand to identify different species that visit your feeders, and watch for different birds' special habits.

Group Activity
• Signs of Winter •

Nature is now preparing for winter. Spend some time with your group discussing and observing this change.

1. Arrange with the children's librarian to get a variety of books on the animal world preparing for winter.

Here are some suggestions:

AUTUMN: DISCOVERING THE SEASONS by Louis Lantrey. Troll Associates, Mahwah, N.J.

FIRST COMES SPRING by Ann Rockwell. Thomas Y. Cromwell, N.Y.

FREDERICK by Leo Lionni. Pantheon, N.Y.

SAY IT by Charlotte Zolotow. Greenwillow Books, N.Y.

SLEEPY BEAR by Lydia Dabcovich. Dutton, N.Y.

THE BIG SNOW by Berta and Elmer Hader. Macmillan, N.Y.

THE KIDS NATURE BOOK by Susan Milord. Williamson Publishing Company, Charlotte, VT.

WINTER NOISY BOOK by Margaret Wise Brown. Harper and Row, N.Y.

2. Discuss the differences between animals and humans preparing for winter.

3. Set up a center with several snowsuits, mittens, winter boots, scarves, and hats. The children can practice putting on outdoor clothing in the proper order.

4. Do a feltboard activity illustrating the change from warm-weather to cold-weather clothing.

5. Place a variety of animal ears in the dramatic play corner where the children can pretend to be animals preparing for winter.

6. Arrange an outing to observe changes in the outdoors.

Game • Alphabet Toss •

You'll need:

• 2 or more laundry baskets
• 26 items whose names begin with each letter of the alphabet

1. Fill one basket with all 26 items.

2. Each child chooses an item and tosses it into the empty basket while saying the initial sound and name of the item.

Creative Activity
• Leafy Splatter Prints •

You'll need:

- painting paper
- newspaper
- tempera paint in plastic containers
- toothbrushes
- autumn leaves

1. Make sure the children, and your table, are well-covered for this one.
2. Place leaves on the painting paper in any pattern. Encourage children not to touch leaves once in place.
3. Dip toothbrushes in paint, point bristles toward the edges of the leaves, and draw thumb along bristles.
4. When finished, lift leaves and note the un-painted pattern they have left behind.
5. These prints can be hung, or saved to make wrapping paper.

Circle Game
• I Went Outside on an Autumn Day •

This sequential game will reinforce what children have learned and read about nature's changes in preparation for winter.

1. The teacher begins by saying," I went outside on an autumn day, and I saw . . ." and adds an observation such as, " . . . children wearing warm hats" or " . . . squirrels gathering food."
2. Each child adds a statement, trying first to remember the previous statement, "I went outside on an autumn day and I saw children wearing warm hats, and apples lying on the ground under the tree."
3. The children continue adding on observations, until the end of the circle is reached.
4. Encourage the children not only to remain quiet while a friend is thinking, but also to help out when necessary.

December Special Event

Kwanzaa, Festival of Light

Every year since 1966, many African Americans have celebrated Kwanzaa from December 26 to January 1. Kwanzaa is a cultural observance founded by Maulana "Ron" Karenga in 1966 to foster African Americans' pride in their African beginnings and culture. The holiday is celebrated from December 26 to January 1 each year and culminates in a feast called the karamu. Kwanzaa is a Swahili word meaning "first fruits of the harvest." Karenga combined elements from many African harvest festivals to create this unique and dynamic celebration.

During Kwanzaa, seven candles are lit, one each day, starting with a black candle, and then alternating between three red candles and three green ones. One of the nguzo saba, or seven principles, is recited and discussed each day in response to the question "What's the news?" or "habari gani?" A good book for children about Kwanzaa is called Kwanzaa, by A. P. Porter, published by Carolrhoda Books, Inc., Minneapolis.

The following are some activities for you to do with children, culminating in the karamu on December 31 or January 1. On this day, zawadi, or small gifts, are given to children as rewards for promises kept during the year.

- Weave placemats, or mkeka, out of red and green strips of paper, woven through a sheet of black paper with slits cut into it. The mkeka will hold the food and drink of the karamu celebration.

- Decorate the room with the African-American flag called a bendera. It has three equal horizontal stripes, red at the top, black in the middle, and green at the bottom.

- Make shakers or drums out of plastic or cardboard containers. Decorate them with red, green, and black symbols, and streamers.

- Have families contribute a kinara, or candle holder, for the mishumaa saba, or seven candles. Put a black candle in the center, three red candles on the left, and three green candles on the right. Bring in an assortment of mazao, or fruits and vegetables, as a harvest symbol. It is traditional to place one ear of corn for each child present on the mkeka. If you have cooking facilities, have children help you prepare a treat such as corn bread for the feast. You will also need a large cup for the unity cup, or kikombe cha umoja, for sipping juice. Sharing from the cup is a symbol of staying together.

- You are now ready for the feast, or karamu. Invite some special guests, and spread the feast on tables on the paper mkeka made by the children. Light the candles, and recite the nguzo saba. Invite an adult to talk about African-American culture, or read an African or African-American folktale. Share the food, and pass the kikombe cha umoja. Use your shakers and drums to celebrate with music. Don't forget to wish each other "Happy Kwanzaa!"

December Activities

Song • My Tree •

(Tune of "My Hat It Has Three Corners")

My tree, it has decorations,
Decorations has my tree,
And had it not decorations,
It would not be my tree.

My dreidel it spins so quickly,
So quickly spins my dreidel,
And did it not spin so quickly,
It would not be my dreidel.

My candles are burning brightly,
Burning brightly are my candles,
And were they not burning brightly,
They would not be my candles.

My reindeer are dashing and prancing,
Dashing and prancing are my reindeer,
And were they not dashing and prancing,
They would not be my reindeer.

Group Activity • Tulip Time in Winter •

Add spring to the February blahs by forcing bulbs now. You'll need a refrigerator or other dark, cool space for 6 to 12 weeks. Be patient; although lengthy, this is a very rewarding activity. To maintain interest, and to observe their development, visit your bulbs once a week and discuss any changes you see.

You'll need:

- recycled plastic plant pots (4" for crocus/hyacinths, 6" for daffodils/tulips)
- potting soil
- fall bulbs (tulip, crocus, daffodil) purchased on sale in late fall
- large spoons
- watering can
- newspaper

1. Cover workspace with newspaper.
2. Each child fills a pot with soil and carefully presses several well-spaced bulbs (of the same variety) on top, "noses" poking up; 1/3 of bulb showing.
3. Mark pots with date, type of bulb, and children's names.
4. Water and place in refrigerator. Don't forget to visit your bulbs weekly to observe their progress.

5. Water only when nearly dry.
6. Within 6–8 weeks for crocus/hyacinth, or 12–14 weeks for tulips/daffodils, the leaves should be well-sprouted (approximately 2–3" long).
7. At this stage, remove pots from fridge, place in indirect light, and continue to water.
8. When flower bud appears, place in a sunny spot, keep watering, and watch your flowers bloom in 3–4 weeks.
9. After leaves have died back completely, remove them (they should come off easily) and plant bulbs in your garden, or keep in a cool place and plant in fall.

Group Activity • Giving Is Fun •

This is a season of giving and sharing for many cultures. Highlight this aspect of the holidays by collecting food for your local food bank, making special crafts or gifts for a nearby children's hospital, or by preparing some songs and snacks for a neighborhood seniors' home. Plan and work on your project well in advance. Try to deliver your gifts in person and be sure to arrange your visit with staff. Plan this activity as the first of many future exchanges.

Creative Activity • Cone Crafts •

These craft ideas add a natural touch to the festive season.

You'll need:

- a collection of pinecones
- glue
- glitter
- play dough
- paper plates
- string
- clothes hangers

1. Dip ends of cones into glue, and sprinkle glitter on them. Tie a string to the top and hang, or hang several from a clothes hanger to create a mobile.
2. Stick several cones into a clump of play dough, let dry, and use as centerpieces. Add evergreen leaves and dried flowers to the arrangements.
3. Make wreaths by cutting out the centers of paper plates, leaving enough of the outer edge to glue on pinecones. Once dry, wrap with narrow ribbon or string to secure the cones.

Recipe • Marzipan Sweets •

This traditional recipe is prepared in the Netherlands to celebrate Sinterklass Avond (St. Nicolas Eve) on December 5.

You'll need:

- 1 1/2 cups whole blanched almonds
- 3/4 cups granulated sugar
- 1 cup confectioners' sugar
- 2 egg whites

1. Blend all ingredients until smooth.
2. Refrigerate until well chilled.
3. Form into small balls; roll in extra confectioners' sugar, if desired.
4. Children can knead orange food coloring into their marzipan, form carrot shapes, and place a clove in the wide end. This symbolizes the carrots people leave in their shoes for St. Nicholas' horse.

Circle Game
• Hanukkah Guessing Game •

After spending time talking about the Hanukkah celebration, play this game.

1. Begin by describing something related to Hanukkah, such as; "I'm made of potatoes, I'm cooked in oil until I'm crunchy and brown, and they put sour cream or applesauce on me. What am I?"
2. Encourage children to keep their responses to themselves until everyone has had time to think.
3. Give each child a turn to describe something.
4. For children who may have difficulty thinking of something, have objects in a bag that they can choose and describe.

SOME FURTHER IDEAS:

• "I have eight candles, plus an extra to do the work, and they light a new one of my candles every night of Hanukkah. What am I?"

• "I look like a little top, I have a Hebrew letter on each one of my four sides, and they use me for a game with nuts. What am I?"

Indoor Activity • Beach Day •

Using a globe, explain that the northern hemisphere's winter season is summer in countries located in the southern hemisphere. Celebrate the southern hemisphere's summer with an indoor beach day!

THINGS TO DO FOR BEACH DAY:

• Wear shorts, T-shirts, or bathing suits over your other clothes.
• Have a picnic. Prepare sandwiches and lemonade, place in a cooler or picnic basket, and serve lunch on a flowered tablecloth spread out on the floor.

• Sing summer songs.
• Blow bubbles.
• Put pails and shovels at sand table.
• Read summer books.
• Put summer puzzles at puzzle table.

Notes

Notes

Notes

Notes